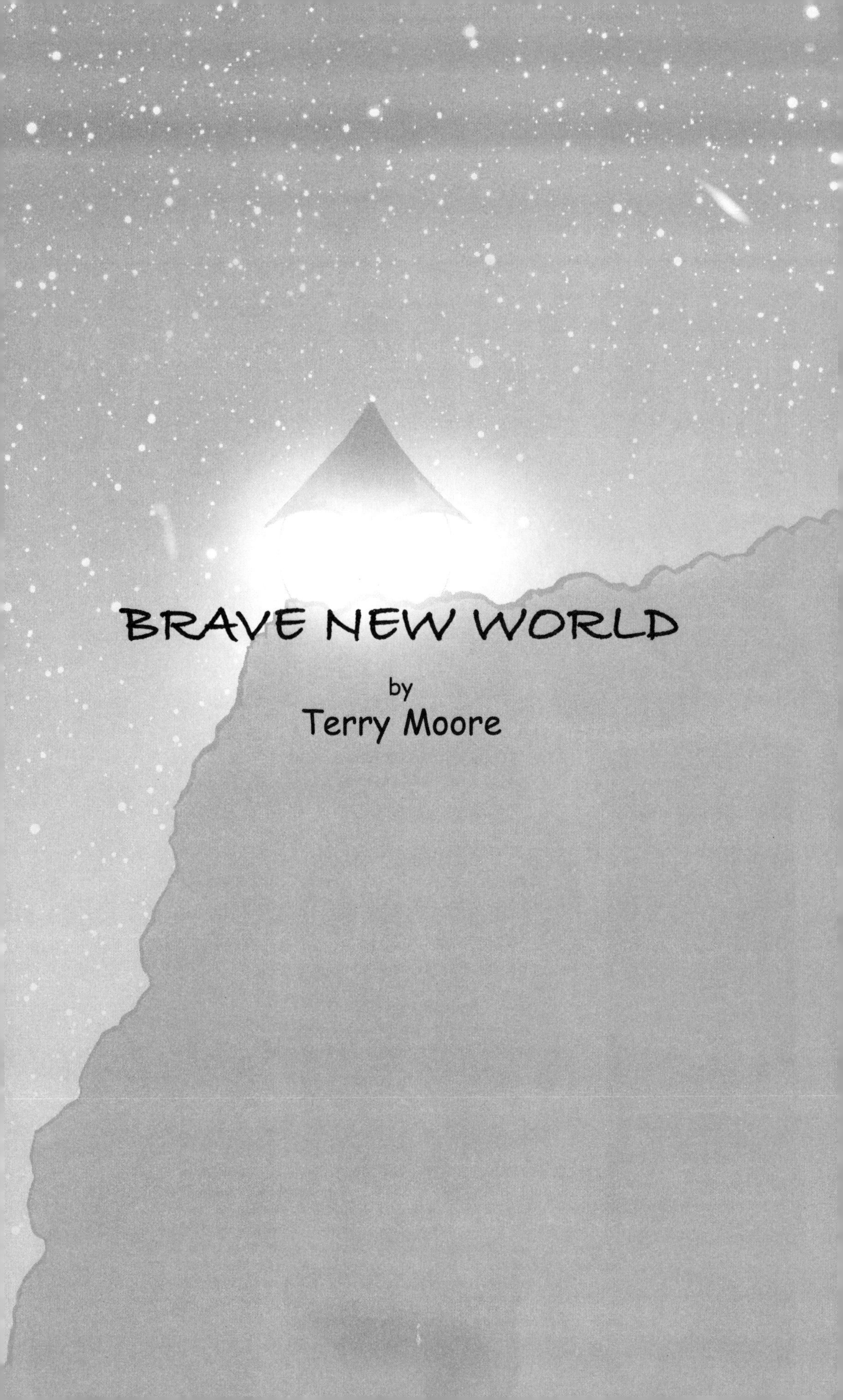

BRAVE NEW WORLD

by
Terry Moore

Special thanks to Jimmy Palmiotti
for his inks on Bare Bones.

STRANGERS IN PARADISE: BRAVE NEW WORLD
Copyright ©2002 Terry Moore
All Rights Reserved

First Edition: July 2002
ISBN 1-892597-16-0

Printed In Canada by Quebecor Printing

Published by
Abstract Studio, Inc.
P. O. Box 271487
Houston, Texas 77277
www.StrangersInParadise.com
email: SIPnet@StrangersInParadise.com

CONTENTS

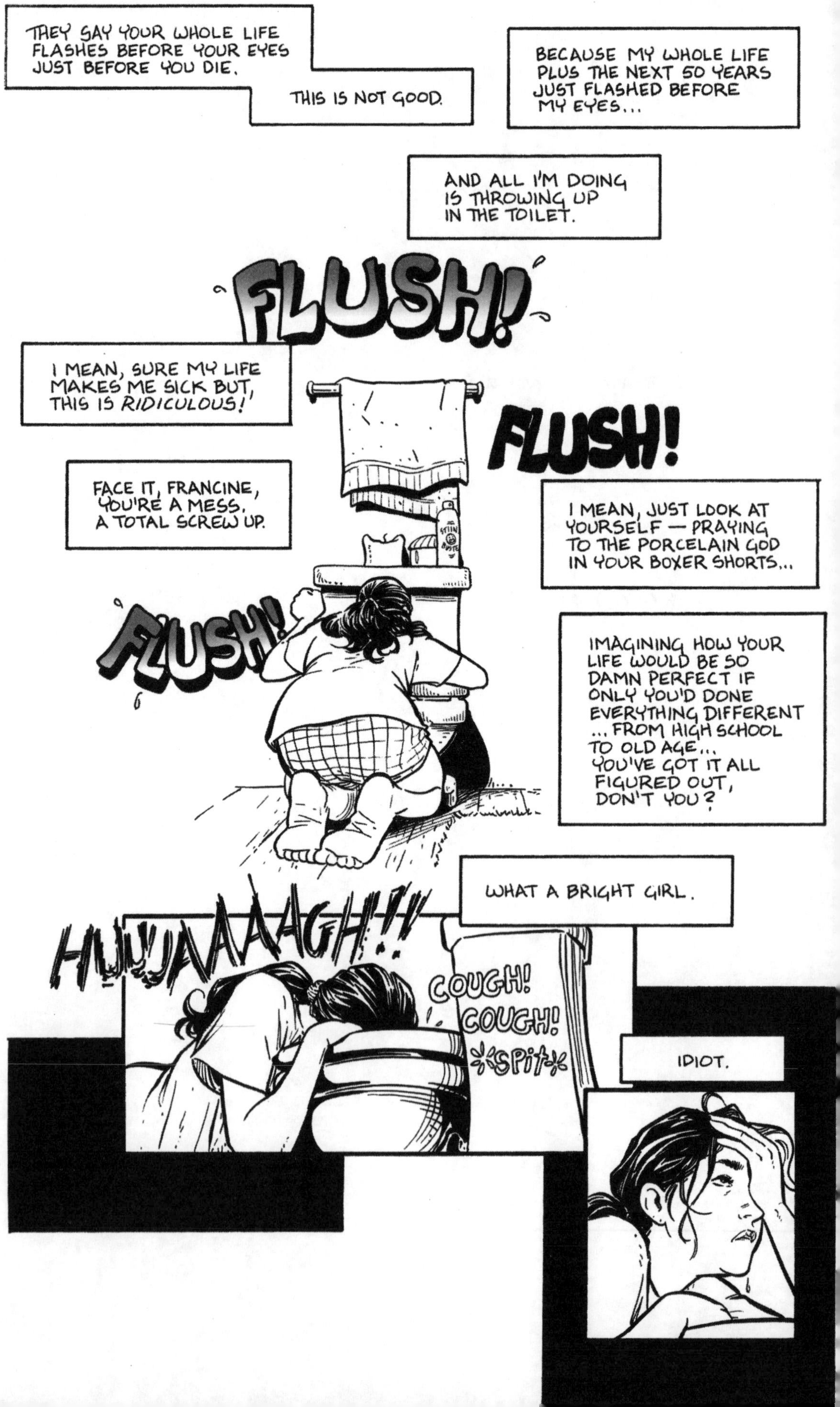

THEY SAY YOUR WHOLE LIFE FLASHES BEFORE YOUR EYES JUST BEFORE YOU DIE.
THIS IS NOT GOOD.
BECAUSE MY WHOLE LIFE PLUS THE NEXT 50 YEARS JUST FLASHED BEFORE MY EYES...
AND ALL I'M DOING IS THROWING UP IN THE TOILET.
FLUSH!
I MEAN, SURE MY LIFE MAKES ME SICK BUT, THIS IS *RIDICULOUS!*
FLUSH!
FACE IT, FRANCINE, YOU'RE A MESS, A TOTAL SCREW UP.
I MEAN, JUST LOOK AT YOURSELF — PRAYING TO THE PORCELAIN GOD IN YOUR BOXER SHORTS...
FLUSH!
IMAGINING HOW YOUR LIFE WOULD BE SO DAMN PERFECT IF ONLY YOU'D DONE EVERYTHING DIFFERENT ... FROM HIGH SCHOOL TO OLD AGE... YOU'VE GOT IT ALL FIGURED OUT, DON'T YOU?
WHAT A BRIGHT GIRL.
HUUUAAAGH!!
COUGH!
COUGH!
SPIT
IDIOT.

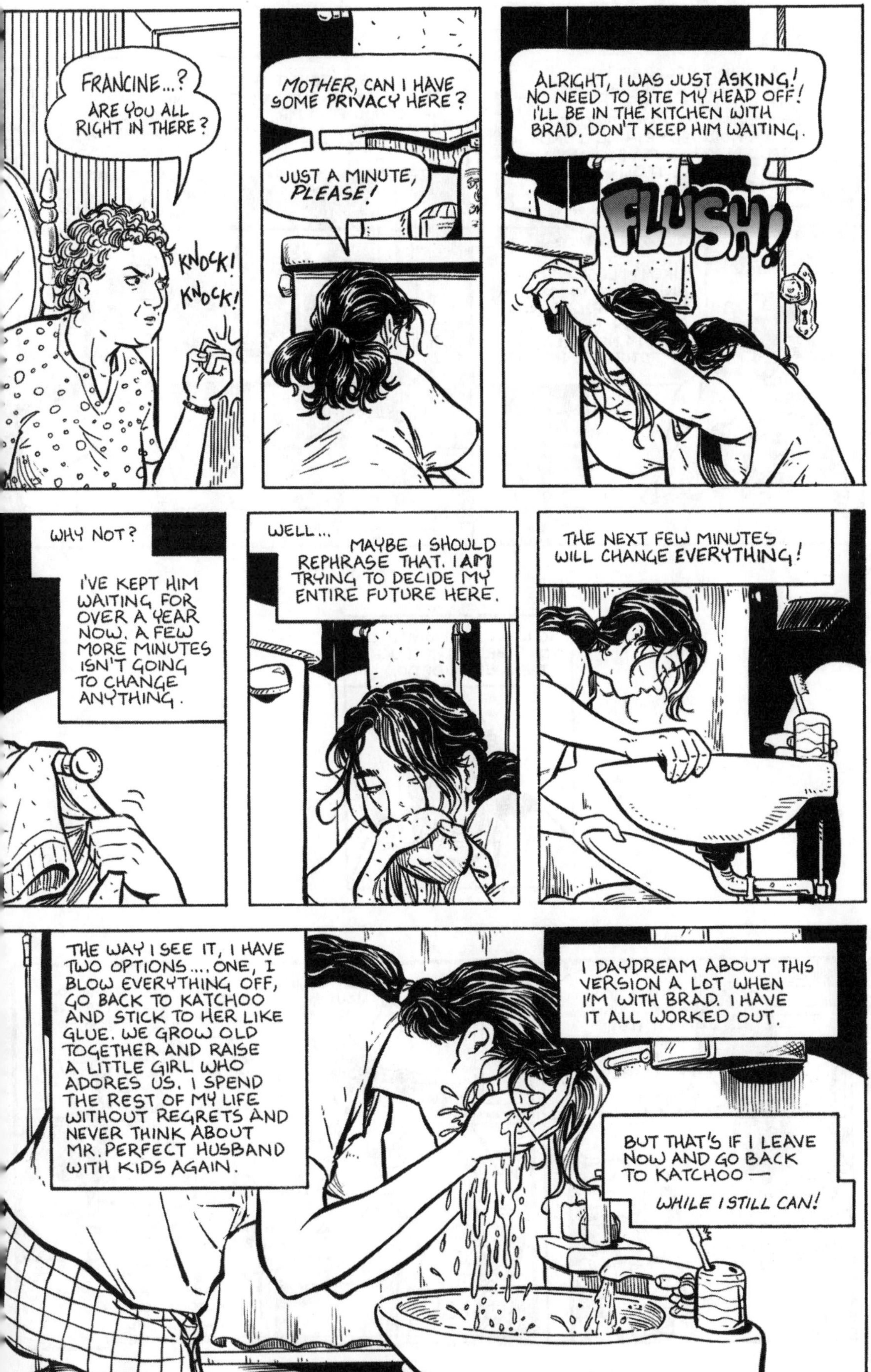
FRANCINE...? ARE YOU ALL RIGHT IN THERE?
KNOCK! KNOCK!
MOTHER, CAN I HAVE SOME PRIVACY HERE?
JUST A MINUTE, PLEASE!
ALRIGHT, I WAS JUST ASKING! NO NEED TO BITE MY HEAD OFF! I'LL BE IN THE KITCHEN WITH BRAD. DON'T KEEP HIM WAITING.
FLUSH!
WHY NOT?
I'VE KEPT HIM WAITING FOR OVER A YEAR NOW. A FEW MORE MINUTES ISN'T GOING TO CHANGE ANYTHING.
WELL...
MAYBE I SHOULD REPHRASE THAT. I AM TRYING TO DECIDE MY ENTIRE FUTURE HERE.
THE NEXT FEW MINUTES WILL CHANGE EVERYTHING!
THE WAY I SEE IT, I HAVE TWO OPTIONS.... ONE, I BLOW EVERYTHING OFF, GO BACK TO KATCHOO AND STICK TO HER LIKE GLUE. WE GROW OLD TOGETHER AND RAISE A LITTLE GIRL WHO ADORES US. I SPEND THE REST OF MY LIFE WITHOUT REGRETS AND NEVER THINK ABOUT MR. PERFECT HUSBAND WITH KIDS AGAIN.
I DAYDREAM ABOUT THIS VERSION A LOT WHEN I'M WITH BRAD. I HAVE IT ALL WORKED OUT.
BUT THAT'S IF I LEAVE NOW AND GO BACK TO KATCHOO—
WHILE I STILL CAN!

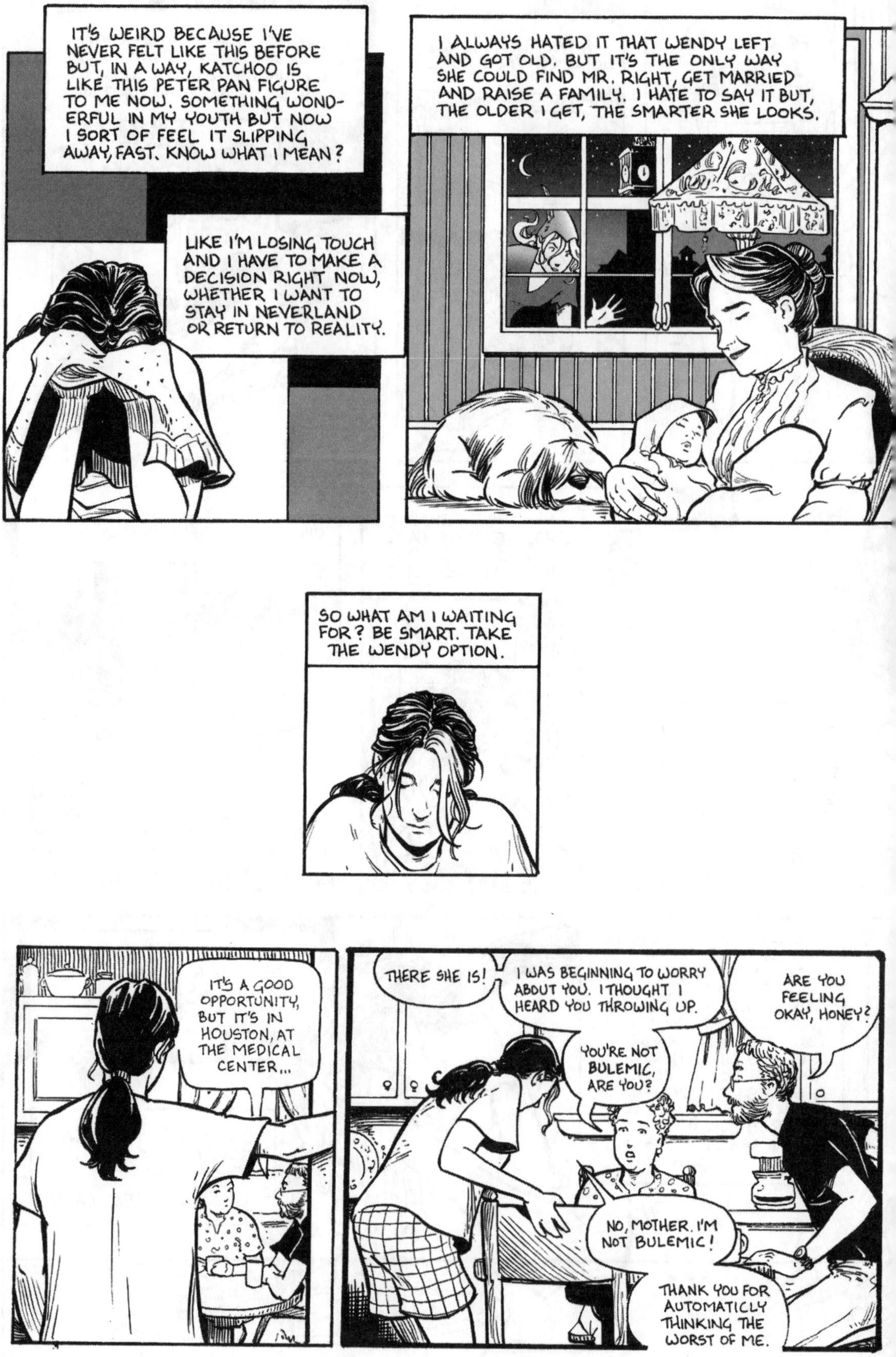
IT'S WEIRD BECAUSE I'VE NEVER FELT LIKE THIS BEFORE BUT, IN A WAY, KATCHOO IS LIKE THIS PETER PAN FIGURE TO ME NOW. SOMETHING WONDERFUL IN MY YOUTH BUT NOW I SORT OF FEEL IT SLIPPING AWAY, FAST. KNOW WHAT I MEAN?
LIKE I'M LOSING TOUCH AND I HAVE TO MAKE A DECISION RIGHT NOW, WHETHER I WANT TO STAY IN NEVERLAND OR RETURN TO REALITY.
I ALWAYS HATED IT THAT WENDY LEFT AND GOT OLD. BUT IT'S THE ONLY WAY SHE COULD FIND MR. RIGHT, GET MARRIED AND RAISE A FAMILY. I HATE TO SAY IT BUT, THE OLDER I GET, THE SMARTER SHE LOOKS.
SO WHAT AM I WAITING FOR? BE SMART. TAKE THE WENDY OPTION.
IT'S A GOOD OPPORTUNITY, BUT IT'S IN HOUSTON, AT THE MEDICAL CENTER...
THERE SHE IS!
I WAS BEGINNING TO WORRY ABOUT YOU. I THOUGHT I HEARD YOU THROWING UP.
ARE YOU FEELING OKAY, HONEY?
YOU'RE NOT BULEMIC, ARE YOU?
NO, MOTHER. I'M NOT BULEMIC!
THANK YOU FOR AUTOMATICLY THINKING THE WORST OF ME.

WHEN A YOUNG WOMAN THROWS UP AFTER BREAKFAST EVERY MORNING, SHE'S EITHER BULEMIC OR....

≥SIGH≤

OH MY WORD! YOU'RE PREGNANT!

WELL, I WAS COMING IN TO TALK TO YOU TWO ABOUT IT BUT... SINCE YOU LET THE CAT OUT OF THE BAG...

YES, I'M PREGNANT.

AAAAEEEEEE!!!!

ARE YOU SERIOUS?

I'M AFRAID SO.

ARE YOU OKAY?

I THINK I NEED TO SIT DOWN.

I DON'T BELIEVE IT! I'M GOING TO BE A GRANDMOTHER!

I'M GOING TO BE A GRANDMOTHER!

GRANDMOTHER IN THE HOUSE!

TRY PUTTING YOUR HEAD BETWEEN YOUR LEGS. I'VE BEEN DOING THAT A LOT LATELY.

DOES IT HELP?

NO. BUT WHY SHOULD I BE THE ONLY ONE?

OH, I CAN'T BELIEVE THIS! WHEN DID YOU FIND OUT?!

HOLY COW

HOLY COW

THIS MORNING. I TOOK A HOME PREGNANCY TEST. I KNEW SOMETHING WAS UP.

HOLY COW

HOLY COW

HOLY COW

HOLY COW

BRAD? ARE YOU OKAY WITH THIS?

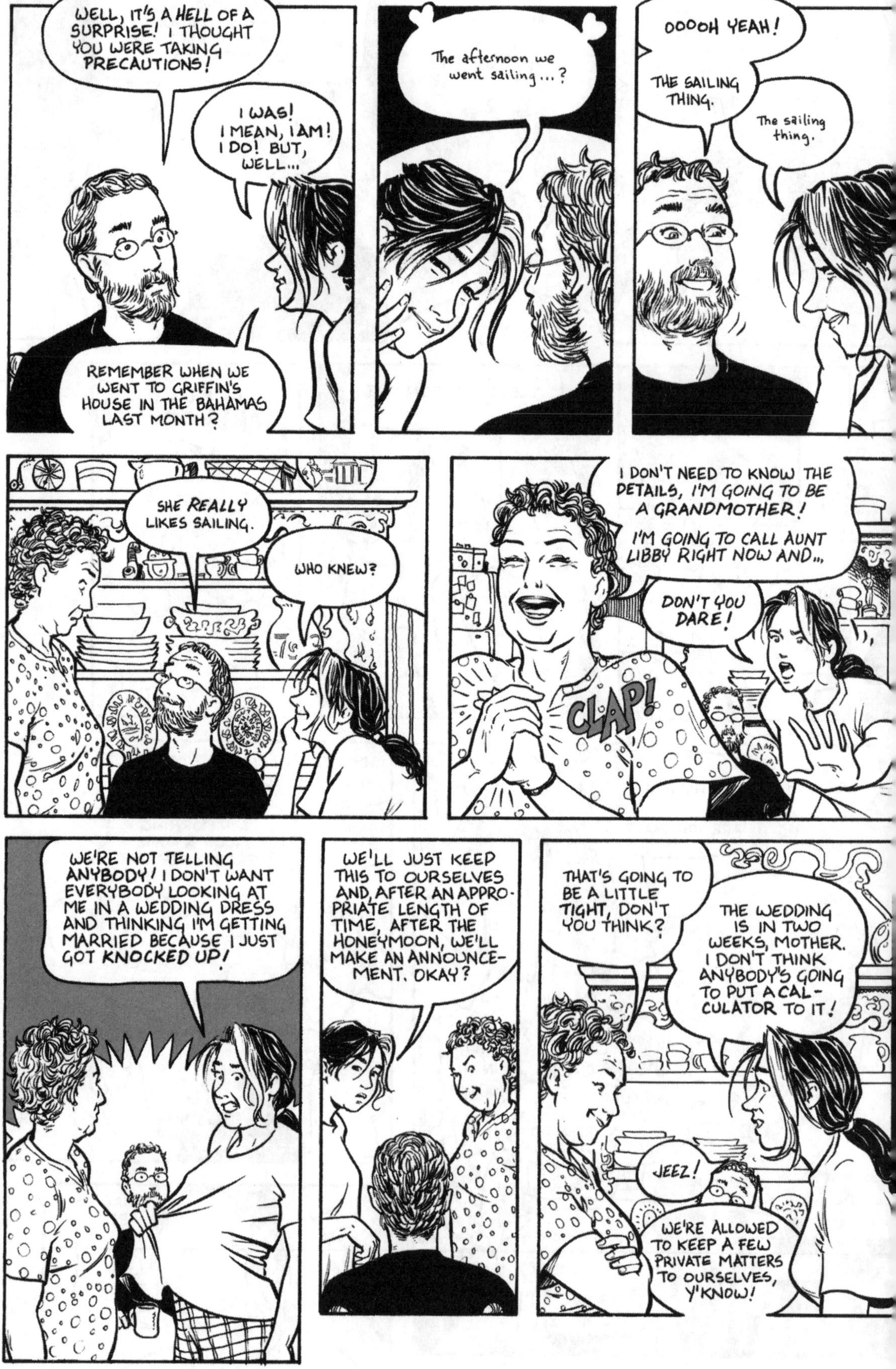

WELL, IT'S A HELL OF A SURPRISE! I THOUGHT YOU WERE TAKING PRECAUTIONS!
I WAS! I MEAN, I AM! I DO! BUT, WELL...
REMEMBER WHEN WE WENT TO GRIFFIN'S HOUSE IN THE BAHAMAS LAST MONTH?
The afternoon we went sailing...?
OOOOH YEAH!
THE SAILING THING.
The sailing thing.
SHE REALLY LIKES SAILING.
WHO KNEW?
I DON'T NEED TO KNOW THE DETAILS, I'M GOING TO BE A GRANDMOTHER!
I'M GOING TO CALL AUNT LIBBY RIGHT NOW AND...
DON'T YOU DARE!
CLAP!
WE'RE NOT TELLING ANYBODY! I DON'T WANT EVERYBODY LOOKING AT ME IN A WEDDING DRESS AND THINKING I'M GETTING MARRIED BECAUSE I JUST GOT KNOCKED UP!
WE'LL JUST KEEP THIS TO OURSELVES AND, AFTER AN APPROPRIATE LENGTH OF TIME, AFTER THE HONEYMOON, WE'LL MAKE AN ANNOUNCEMENT. OKAY?
THAT'S GOING TO BE A LITTLE TIGHT, DON'T YOU THINK?
THE WEDDING IS IN TWO WEEKS, MOTHER. I DON'T THINK ANYBODY'S GOING TO PUT A CALCULATOR TO IT!
JEEZ!
WE'RE ALLOWED TO KEEP A FEW PRIVATE MATTERS TO OURSELVES, Y'KNOW!

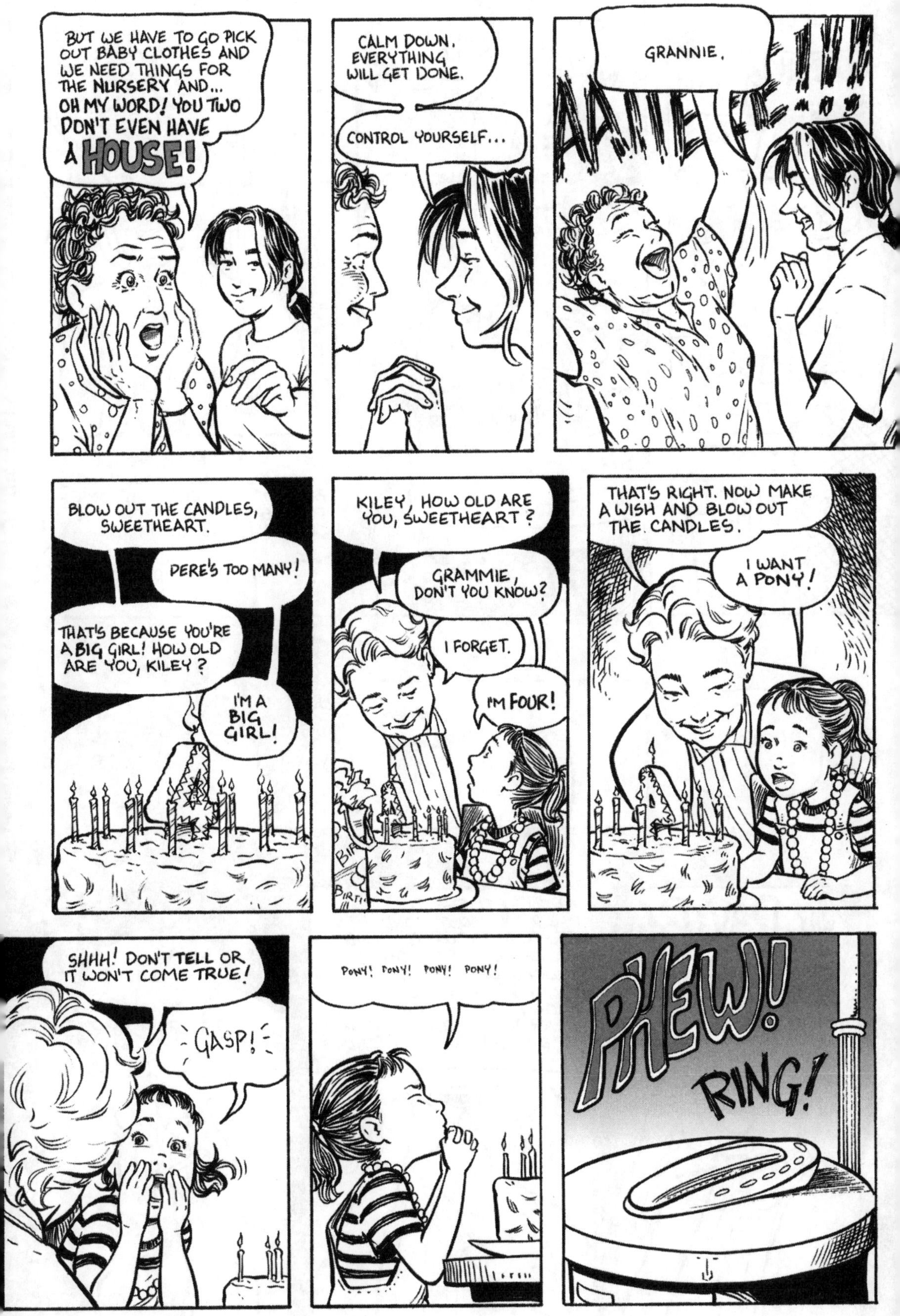
BUT WE HAVE TO GO PICK OUT BABY CLOTHES AND WE NEED THINGS FOR THE NURSERY AND... OH MY WORD! YOU TWO DON'T EVEN HAVE A HOUSE!
CALM DOWN. EVERYTHING WILL GET DONE.
CONTROL YOURSELF...
GRANNIE.
AAIIEEEE!!!
BLOW OUT THE CANDLES, SWEETHEART.
DERE'S TOO MANY!
THAT'S BECAUSE YOU'RE A BIG GIRL! HOW OLD ARE YOU, KILEY?
I'M A BIG GIRL!
KILEY, HOW OLD ARE YOU, SWEETHEART?
GRAMMIE, DON'T YOU KNOW?
I FORGET.
I'M FOUR!
THAT'S RIGHT. NOW MAKE A WISH AND BLOW OUT THE CANDLES.
I WANT A PONY!
SHHH! DON'T TELL OR IT WON'T COME TRUE!
GASP!
PONY! PONY! PONY! PONY!
PHEW!
RING!

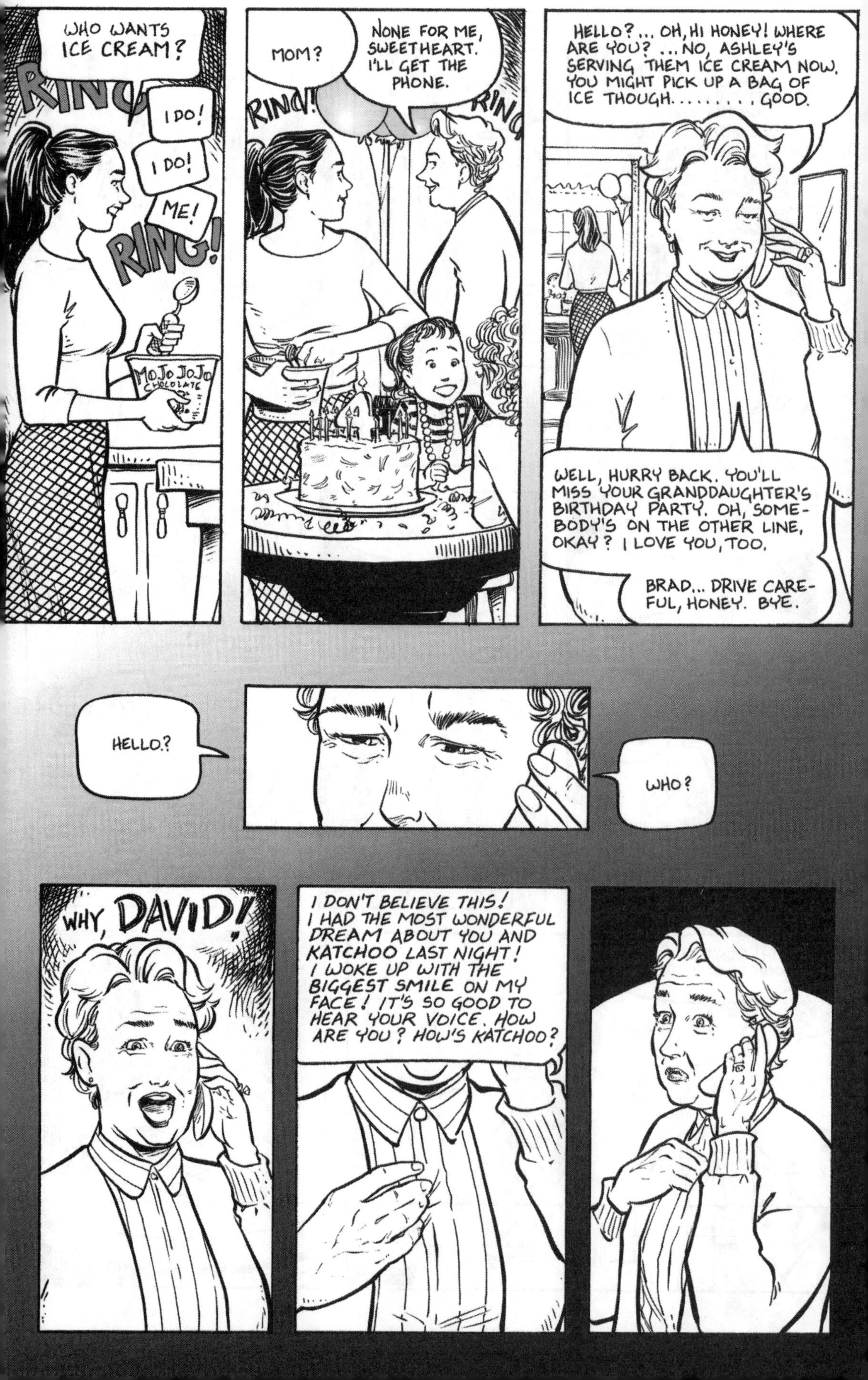
WHO WANTS ICE CREAM?
RING
I DO!
I DO!
ME!
RING!
MOJO JOJO CHOCOLATE
MOM?
NONE FOR ME, SWEETHEART. I'LL GET THE PHONE.
RING!
RING
HELLO?... OH, HI HONEY! WHERE ARE YOU? ...NO, ASHLEY'S SERVING THEM ICE CREAM NOW. YOU MIGHT PICK UP A BAG OF ICE THOUGH.........GOOD.
WELL, HURRY BACK. YOU'LL MISS YOUR GRANDDAUGHTER'S BIRTHDAY PARTY. OH, SOMEBODY'S ON THE OTHER LINE, OKAY? I LOVE YOU, TOO.
BRAD... DRIVE CAREFUL, HONEY. BYE.
HELLO.?
WHO?
WHY, DAVID!
I DON'T BELIEVE THIS! I HAD THE MOST WONDERFUL DREAM ABOUT YOU AND KATCHOO LAST NIGHT! I WOKE UP WITH THE BIGGEST SMILE ON MY FACE! IT'S SO GOOD TO HEAR YOUR VOICE. HOW ARE YOU? HOW'S KATCHOO?

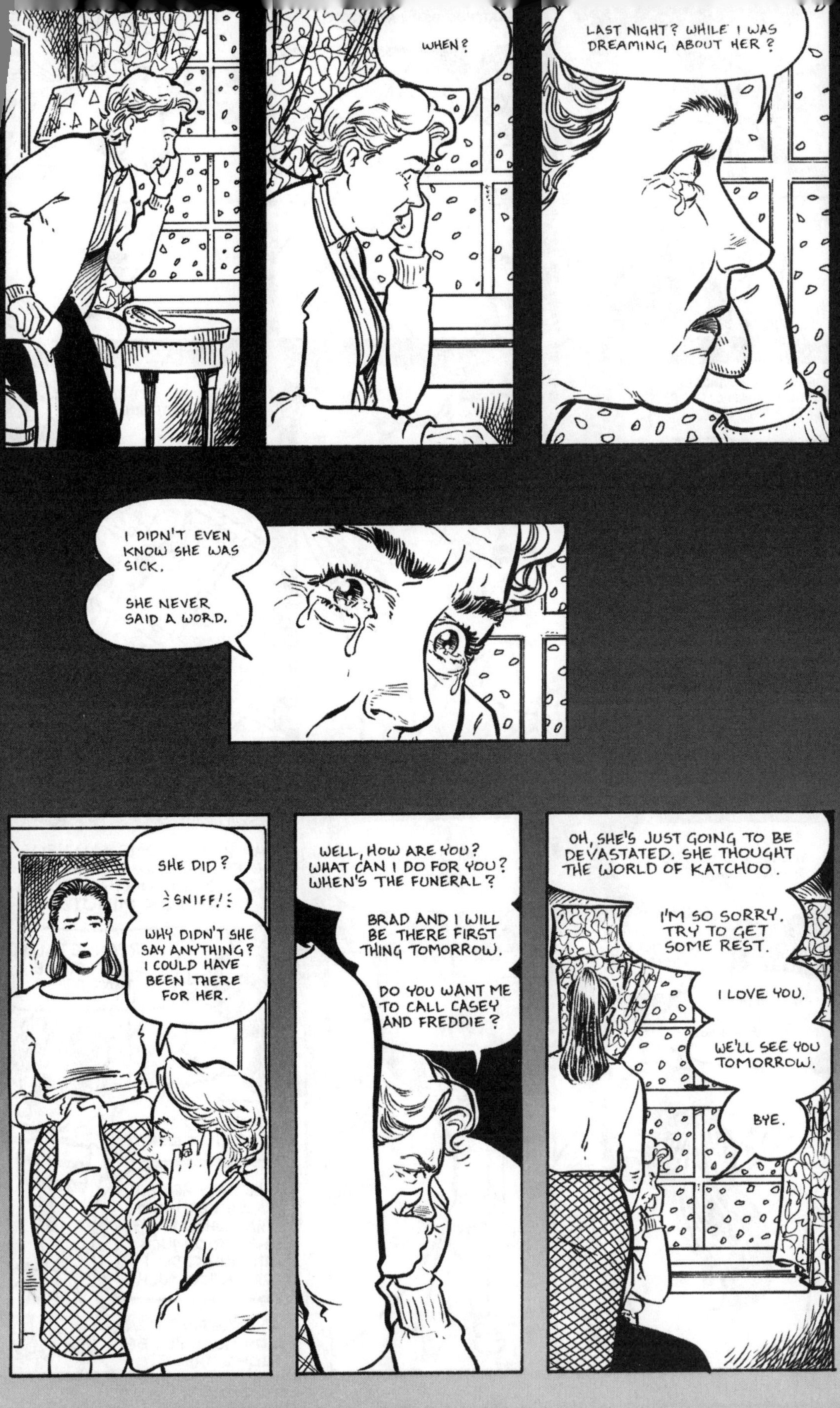

WHEN?
LAST NIGHT? WHILE I WAS DREAMING ABOUT HER?
I DIDN'T EVEN KNOW SHE WAS SICK.
SHE NEVER SAID A WORD.
SHE DID?
SNIFF!
WHY DIDN'T SHE SAY ANYTHING? I COULD HAVE BEEN THERE FOR HER.
WELL, HOW ARE YOU? WHAT CAN I DO FOR YOU? WHEN'S THE FUNERAL?
BRAD AND I WILL BE THERE FIRST THING TOMORROW.
DO YOU WANT ME TO CALL CASEY AND FREDDIE?
OH, SHE'S JUST GOING TO BE DEVASTATED. SHE THOUGHT THE WORLD OF KATCHOO.
I'M SO SORRY. TRY TO GET SOME REST.
I LOVE YOU.
WE'LL SEE YOU TOMORROW.
BYE.

MOM?

KATCHOO DIED LAST NIGHT.

OH MOTHER... I'M SO SORRY.

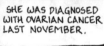

SHE WAS DIAGNOSED WITH OVARIAN CANCER LAST NOVEMBER.

SHE DIDN'T TELL ME.

I NEVER GOT TO SAY GOODBYE.

≈SOB≈

THERE ARE SO MANY THINGS I WANTED TO TELL HER....

AND NOW IT'S TOO LATE!

SHE KNOWS HOW YOU FEEL, MOM. SHE KNOWS.

WHAT'S WRONG WITH GRAMMIE?

SHE HEARD SOME BAD NEWS ABOUT A FRIEND, HONEY. GO BACK TO THE PARTY — I'LL BE THERE IN A MINUTE.

MARYANNE CALLED ME A FLOOSIE. IS THAT BAD?

WHERE DID SHE HEAR THAT WORD?

SHE SAYS HER DAD CALLS HER MOM THAT WHEN SHE'S HAD TOO MUCH TO DRINK. DO I DRINK TOO MUCH?

NO, YOU'RE FINE, DEAR. GO ON NOW, I'LL BE RIGHT THERE.

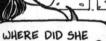

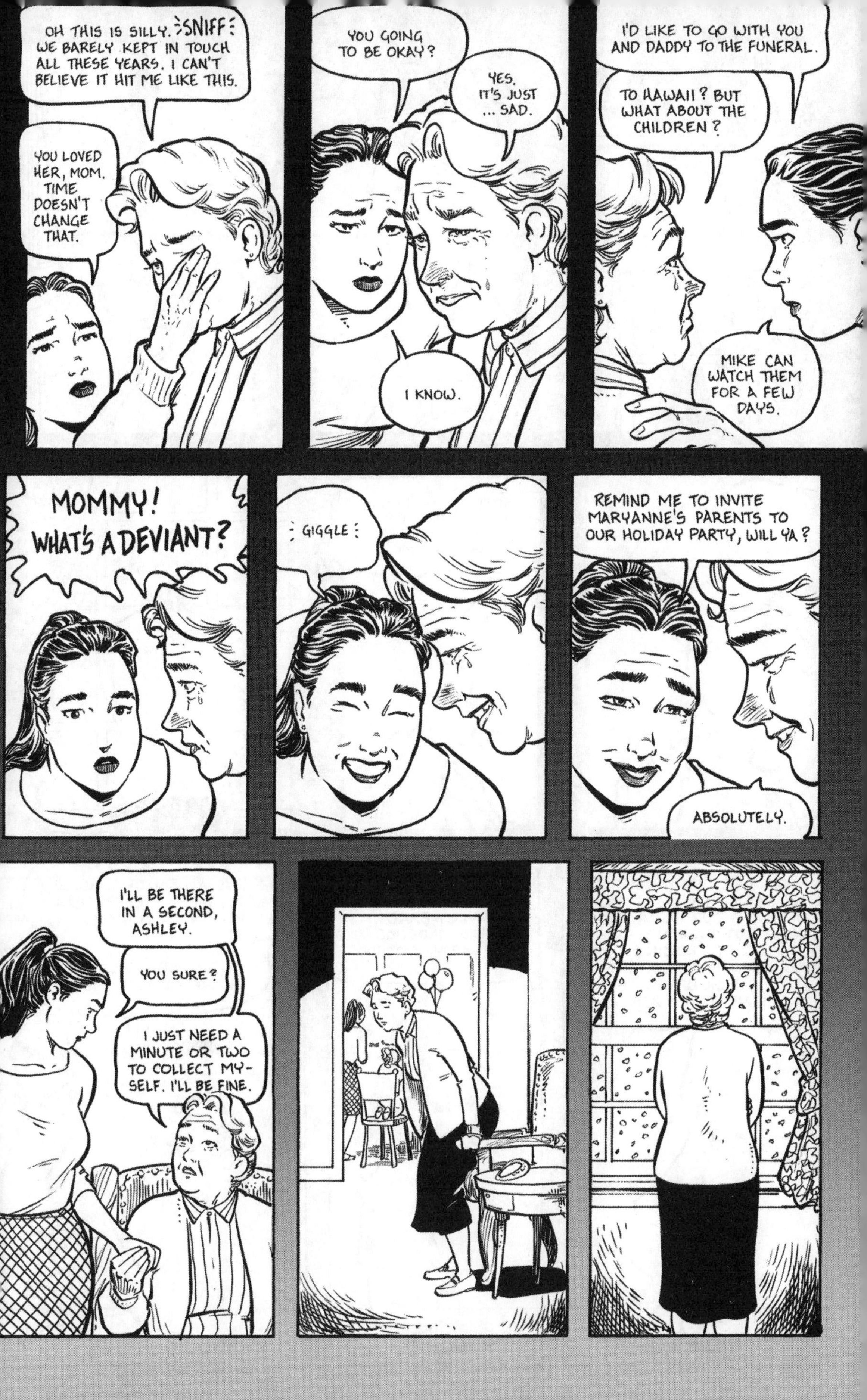

OH THIS IS SILLY. SNIFF WE BARELY KEPT IN TOUCH ALL THESE YEARS. I CAN'T BELIEVE IT HIT ME LIKE THIS.
YOU LOVED HER, MOM. TIME DOESN'T CHANGE THAT.
YOU GOING TO BE OKAY?
YES. IT'S JUST ... SAD.
I KNOW.
I'D LIKE TO GO WITH YOU AND DADDY TO THE FUNERAL.
TO HAWAII? BUT WHAT ABOUT THE CHILDREN?
MIKE CAN WATCH THEM FOR A FEW DAYS.
MOMMY! WHAT'S A DEVIANT?
GIGGLE
REMIND ME TO INVITE MARYANNE'S PARENTS TO OUR HOLIDAY PARTY, WILL YA?
ABSOLUTELY.
I'LL BE THERE IN A SECOND, ASHLEY.
YOU SURE?
I JUST NEED A MINUTE OR TWO TO COLLECT MY-SELF. I'LL BE FINE.

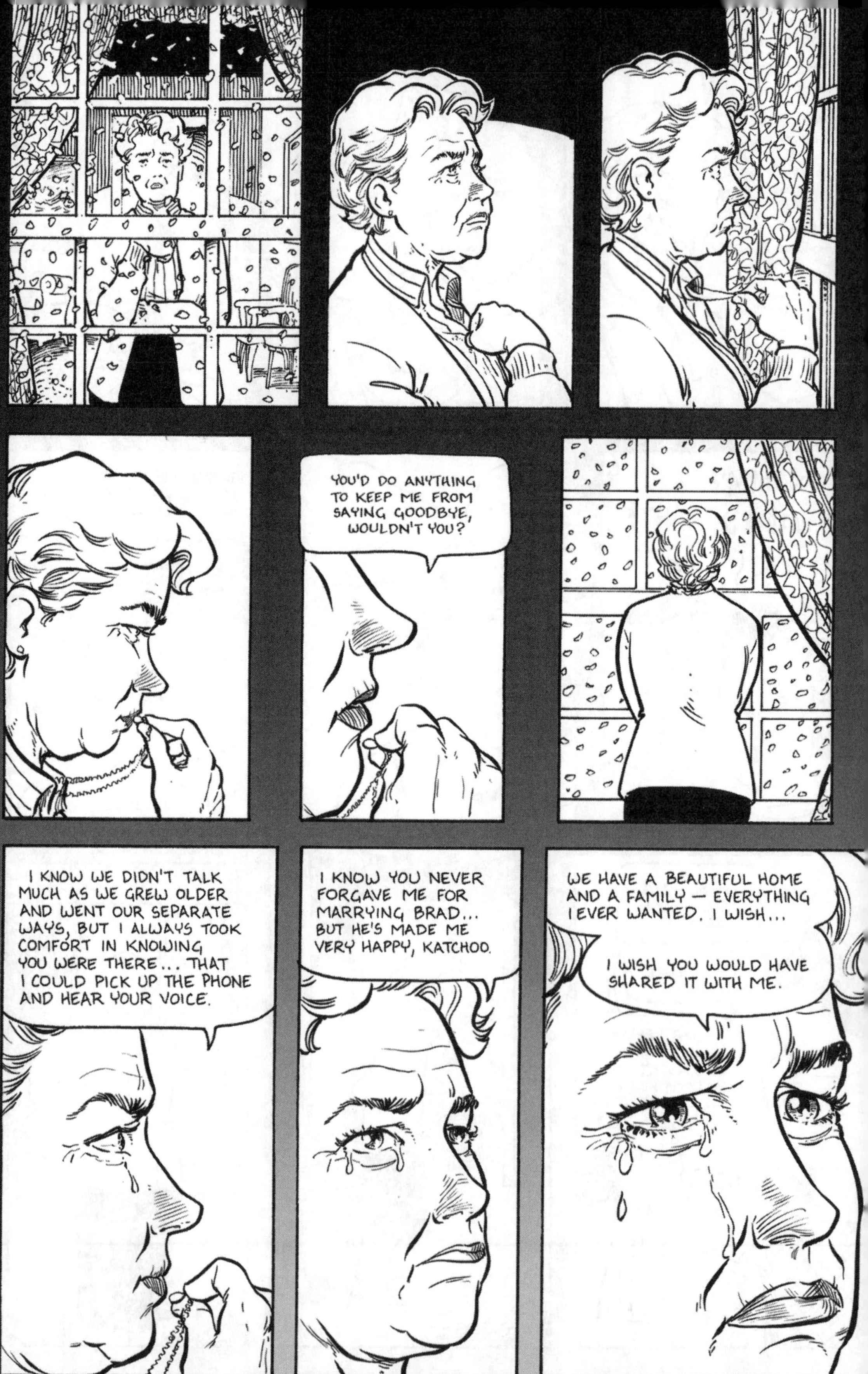
YOU'D DO ANYTHING TO KEEP ME FROM SAYING GOODBYE, WOULDN'T YOU?
I KNOW WE DIDN'T TALK MUCH AS WE GREW OLDER AND WENT OUR SEPARATE WAYS, BUT I ALWAYS TOOK COMFORT IN KNOWING YOU WERE THERE... THAT I COULD PICK UP THE PHONE AND HEAR YOUR VOICE.
I KNOW YOU NEVER FORGAVE ME FOR MARRYING BRAD... BUT HE'S MADE ME VERY HAPPY, KATCHOO.
WE HAVE A BEAUTIFUL HOME AND A FAMILY — EVERYTHING I EVER WANTED. I WISH...
I WISH YOU WOULD HAVE SHARED IT WITH ME.

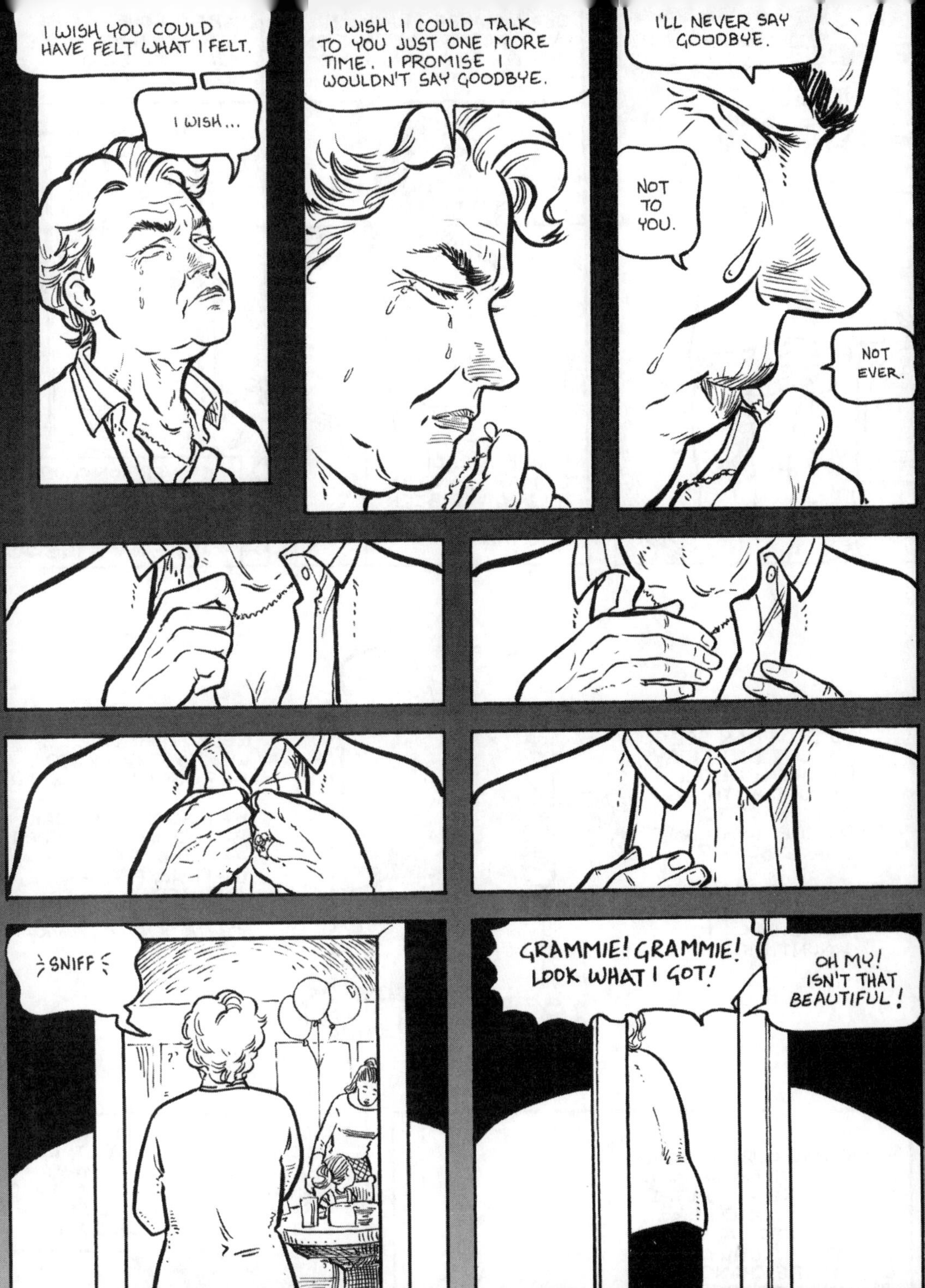
I WISH YOU COULD HAVE FELT WHAT I FELT.
I WISH...
I WISH I COULD TALK TO YOU JUST ONE MORE TIME. I PROMISE I WOULDN'T SAY GOODBYE.
I'LL NEVER SAY GOODBYE.
NOT TO YOU.
NOT EVER.
SNIFF
GRAMMIE! GRAMMIE! LOOK WHAT I GOT!
OH MY! ISN'T THAT BEAUTIFUL!

The End

... of Version Two

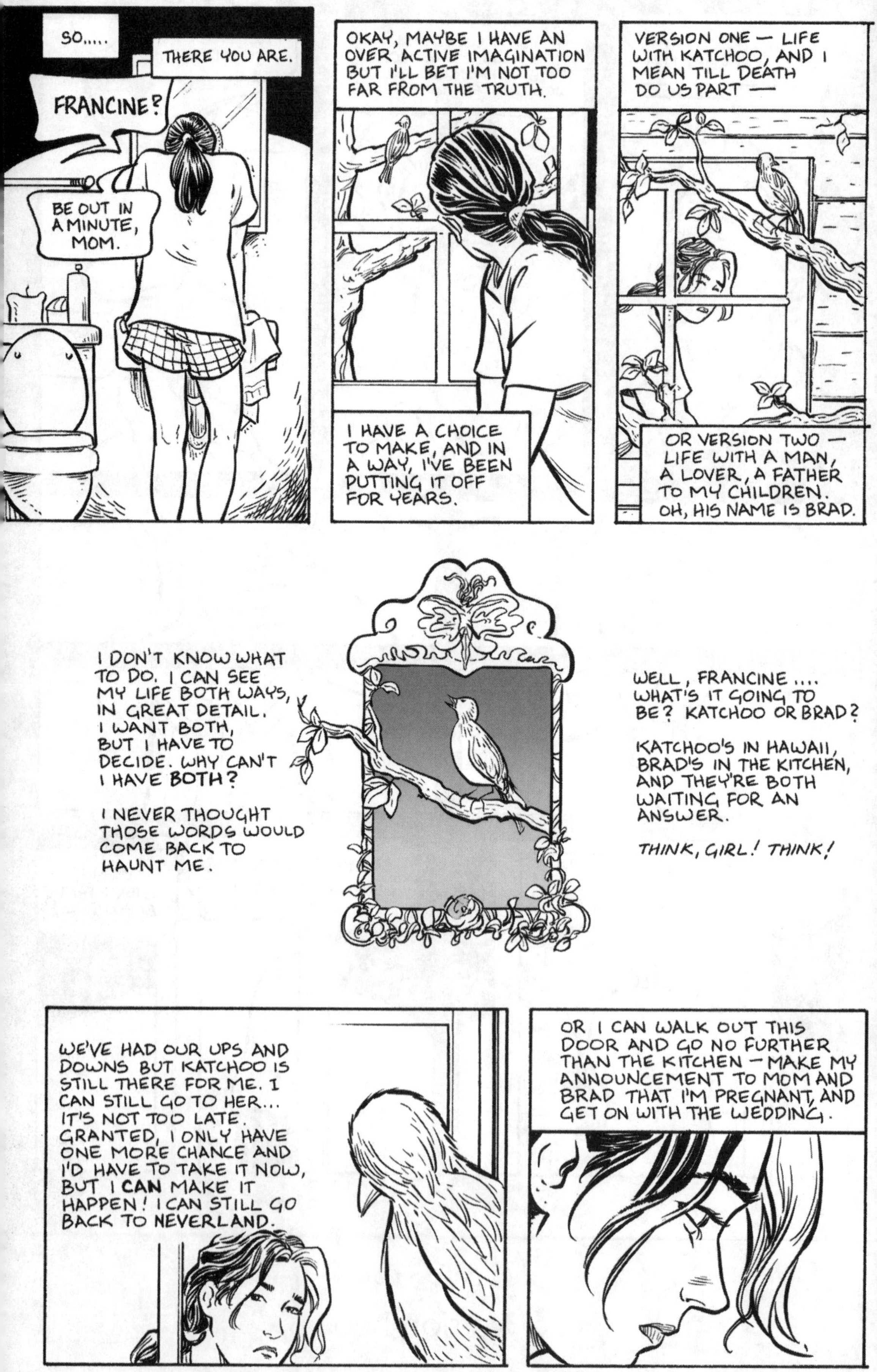
SO.....
THERE YOU ARE.
FRANCINE?
BE OUT IN A MINUTE, MOM.
OKAY, MAYBE I HAVE AN OVER ACTIVE IMAGINATION BUT I'LL BET I'M NOT TOO FAR FROM THE TRUTH.
I HAVE A CHOICE TO MAKE, AND IN A WAY, I'VE BEEN PUTTING IT OFF FOR YEARS.
VERSION ONE — LIFE WITH KATCHOO, AND I MEAN TILL DEATH DO US PART —
OR VERSION TWO — LIFE WITH A MAN, A LOVER, A FATHER TO MY CHILDREN. OH, HIS NAME IS BRAD.
I DON'T KNOW WHAT TO DO. I CAN SEE MY LIFE BOTH WAYS, IN GREAT DETAIL. I WANT BOTH, BUT I HAVE TO DECIDE. WHY CAN'T I HAVE **BOTH**?
I NEVER THOUGHT THOSE WORDS WOULD COME BACK TO HAUNT ME.
WELL, FRANCINE .... WHAT'S IT GOING TO BE? KATCHOO OR BRAD?
KATCHOO'S IN HAWAII, BRAD'S IN THE KITCHEN, AND THEY'RE BOTH WAITING FOR AN ANSWER.
THINK, GIRL! THINK!
WE'VE HAD OUR UPS AND DOWNS BUT KATCHOO IS STILL THERE FOR ME. I CAN STILL GO TO HER... IT'S NOT TOO LATE. GRANTED, I ONLY HAVE ONE MORE CHANCE AND I'D HAVE TO TAKE IT NOW, BUT I **CAN** MAKE IT HAPPEN! I CAN STILL GO BACK TO **NEVERLAND**.
OR I CAN WALK OUT THIS DOOR AND GO NO FURTHER THAN THE KITCHEN — MAKE MY ANNOUNCEMENT TO MOM AND BRAD THAT I'M PREGNANT, AND GET ON WITH THE WEDDING.

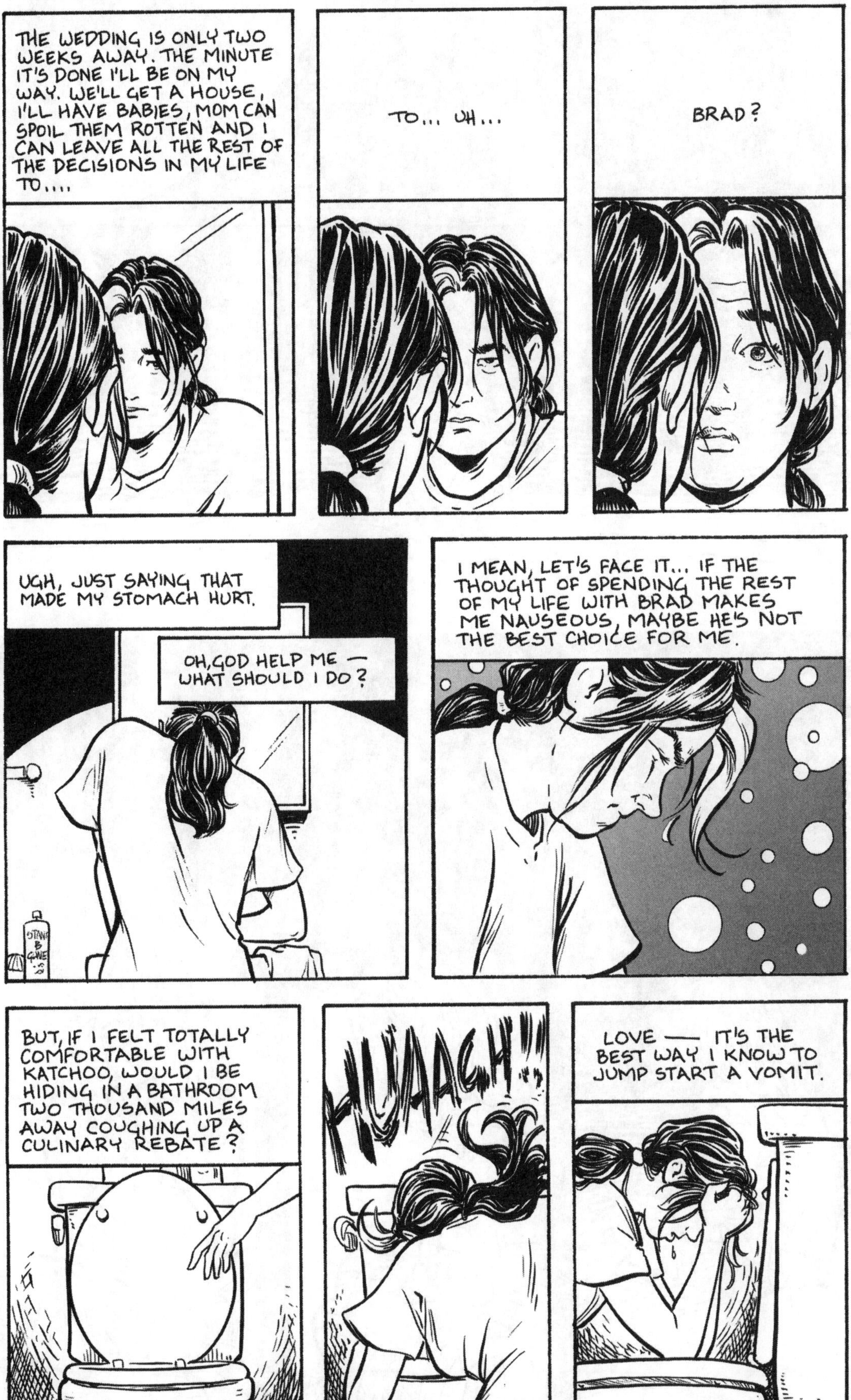
THE WEDDING IS ONLY TWO WEEKS AWAY. THE MINUTE IT'S DONE I'LL BE ON MY WAY. WE'LL GET A HOUSE, I'LL HAVE BABIES, MOM CAN SPOIL THEM ROTTEN AND I CAN LEAVE ALL THE REST OF THE DECISIONS IN MY LIFE TO....
TO... UH...
BRAD?
UGH, JUST SAYING THAT MADE MY STOMACH HURT.
OH, GOD HELP ME — WHAT SHOULD I DO?
I MEAN, LET'S FACE IT... IF THE THOUGHT OF SPENDING THE REST OF MY LIFE WITH BRAD MAKES ME NAUSEOUS, MAYBE HE'S NOT THE BEST CHOICE FOR ME.
BUT, IF I FELT TOTALLY COMFORTABLE WITH KATCHOO, WOULD I BE HIDING IN A BATHROOM TWO THOUSAND MILES AWAY COUGHING UP A CULINARY REBATE?
HUAACH!!
LOVE — IT'S THE BEST WAY I KNOW TO JUMP START A VOMIT.

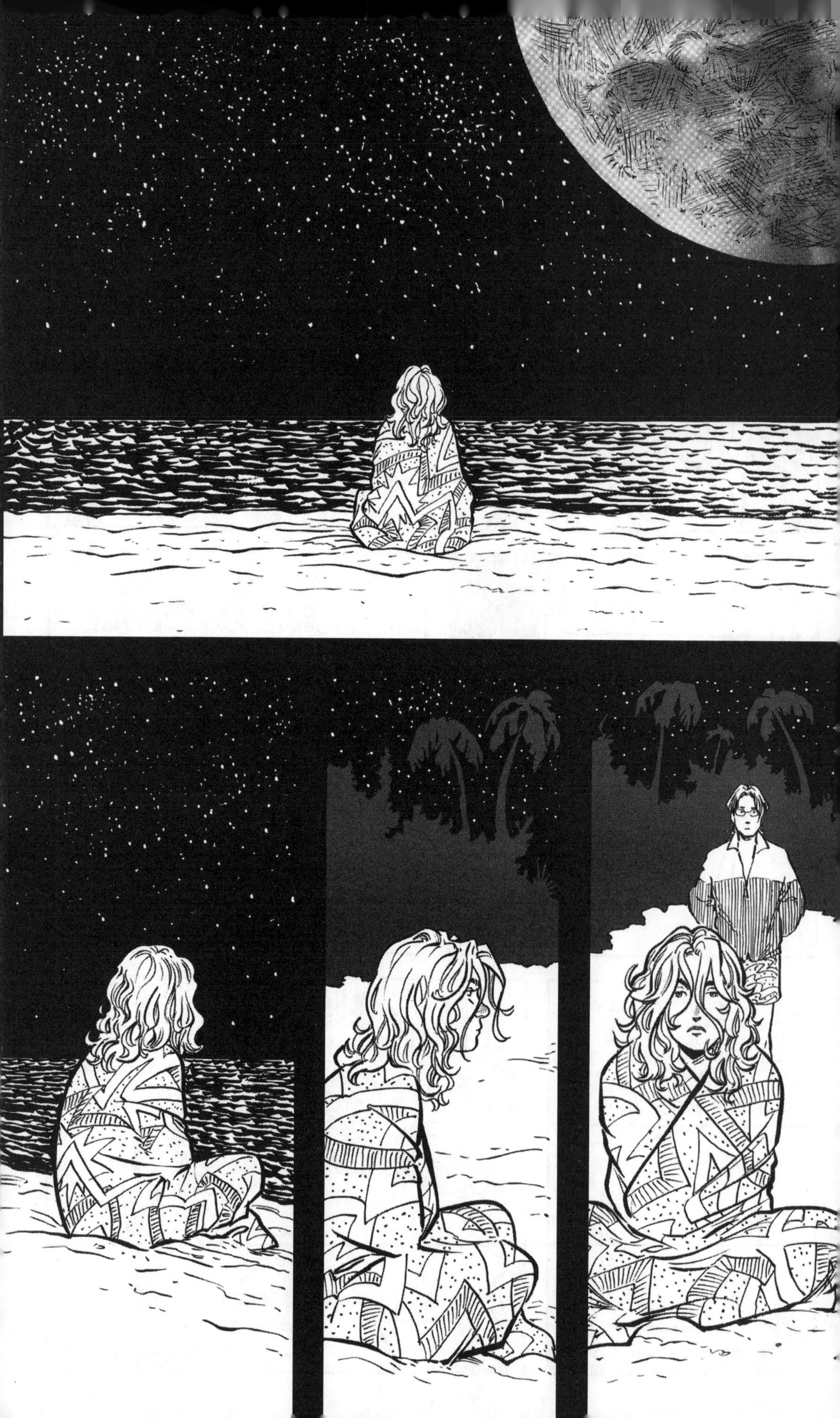

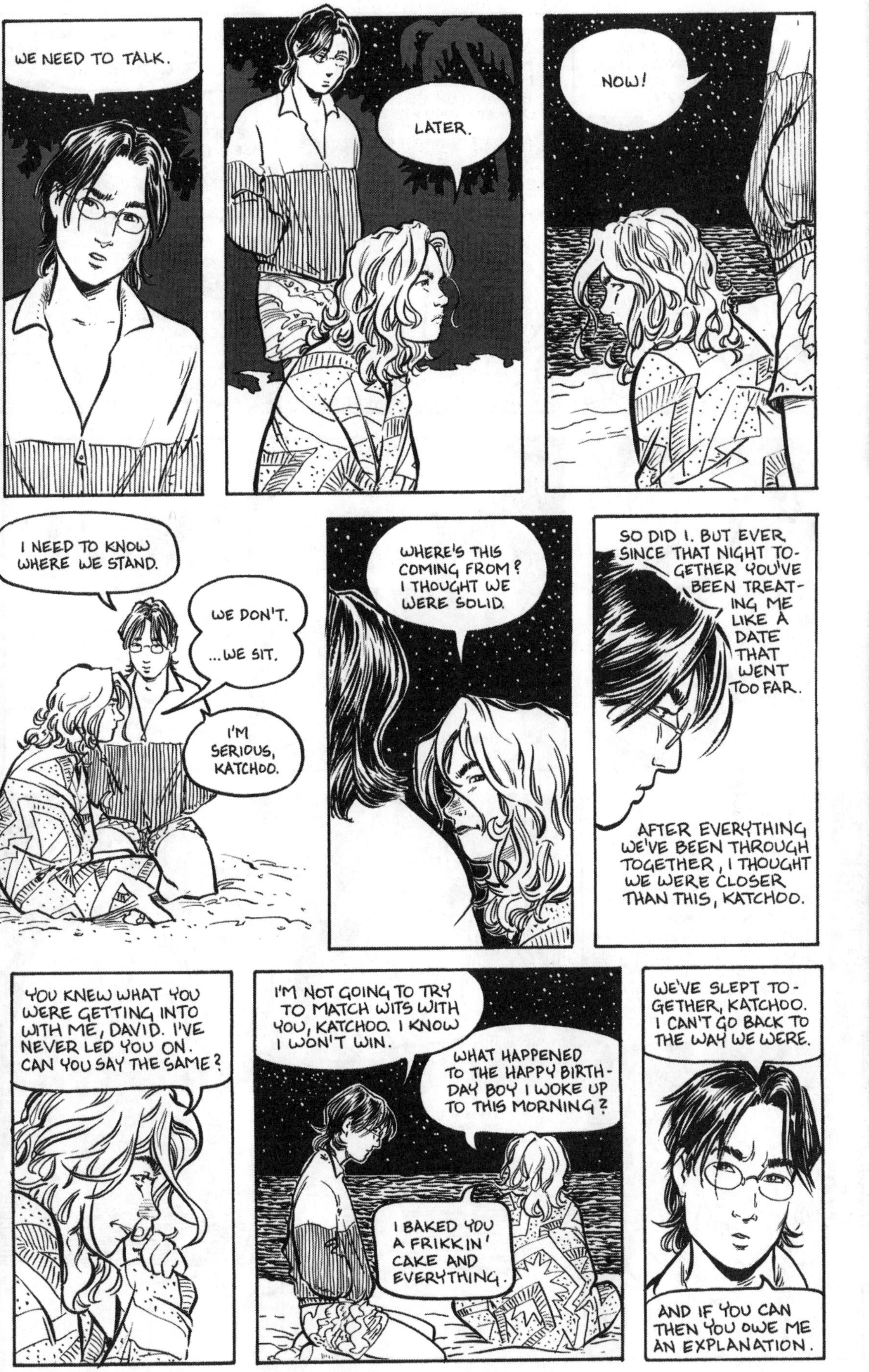
WE NEED TO TALK.
LATER.
NOW!
I NEED TO KNOW WHERE WE STAND.
WE DON'T.
...WE SIT.
I'M SERIOUS, KATCHOO.
WHERE'S THIS COMING FROM? I THOUGHT WE WERE SOLID.
SO DID I. BUT EVER SINCE THAT NIGHT TOGETHER YOU'VE BEEN TREATING ME LIKE A DATE THAT WENT TOO FAR.
AFTER EVERYTHING WE'VE BEEN THROUGH TOGETHER, I THOUGHT WE WERE CLOSER THAN THIS, KATCHOO.
YOU KNEW WHAT YOU WERE GETTING INTO WITH ME, DAVID. I'VE NEVER LED YOU ON. CAN YOU SAY THE SAME?
I'M NOT GOING TO TRY TO MATCH WITS WITH YOU, KATCHOO. I KNOW I WON'T WIN.
WHAT HAPPENED TO THE HAPPY BIRTHDAY BOY I WOKE UP TO THIS MORNING?
I BAKED YOU A FRIKKIN' CAKE AND EVERYTHING.
WE'VE SLEPT TOGETHER, KATCHOO. I CAN'T GO BACK TO THE WAY WE WERE.
AND IF YOU CAN THEN YOU OWE ME AN EXPLANATION.

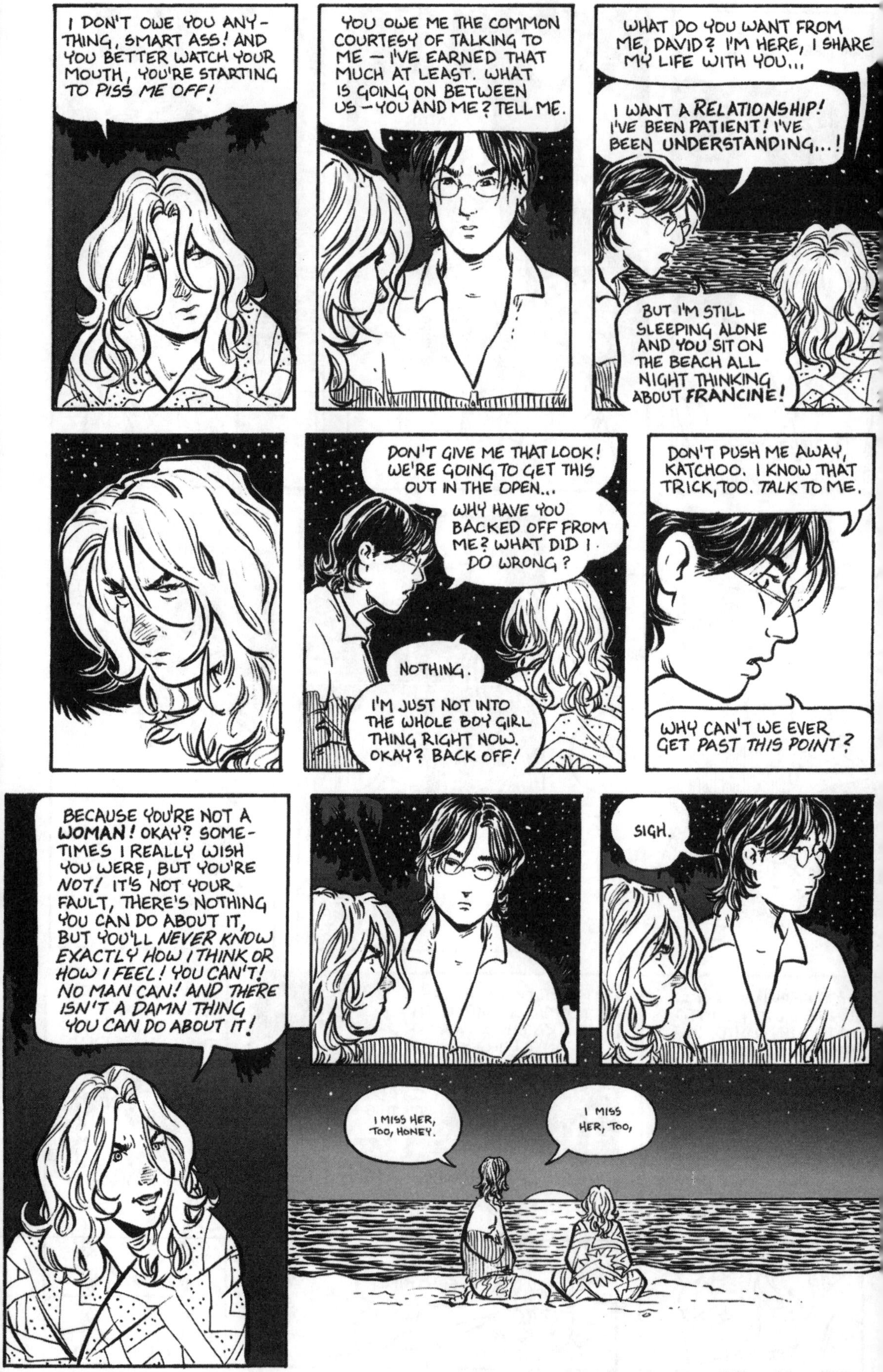
I DON'T OWE YOU ANYTHING, SMART ASS! AND YOU BETTER WATCH YOUR MOUTH, YOU'RE STARTING TO PISS ME OFF!
YOU OWE ME THE COMMON COURTESY OF TALKING TO ME — I'VE EARNED THAT MUCH AT LEAST. WHAT IS GOING ON BETWEEN US — YOU AND ME? TELL ME.
WHAT DO YOU WANT FROM ME, DAVID? I'M HERE, I SHARE MY LIFE WITH YOU...
I WANT A RELATIONSHIP! I'VE BEEN PATIENT! I'VE BEEN UNDERSTANDING...!
BUT I'M STILL SLEEPING ALONE AND YOU SIT ON THE BEACH ALL NIGHT THINKING ABOUT FRANCINE!
DON'T GIVE ME THAT LOOK! WE'RE GOING TO GET THIS OUT IN THE OPEN...
WHY HAVE YOU BACKED OFF FROM ME? WHAT DID I DO WRONG?
NOTHING.
I'M JUST NOT INTO THE WHOLE BOY GIRL THING RIGHT NOW. OKAY? BACK OFF!
DON'T PUSH ME AWAY, KATCHOO. I KNOW THAT TRICK, TOO. TALK TO ME.
WHY CAN'T WE EVER GET PAST THIS POINT?
BECAUSE YOU'RE NOT A WOMAN! OKAY? SOMETIMES I REALLY WISH YOU WERE, BUT YOU'RE NOT! IT'S NOT YOUR FAULT, THERE'S NOTHING YOU CAN DO ABOUT IT, BUT YOU'LL NEVER KNOW EXACTLY HOW I THINK OR HOW I FEEL! YOU CAN'T! NO MAN CAN! AND THERE ISN'T A DAMN THING YOU CAN DO ABOUT IT!
SIGH.
I MISS HER, TOO, HONEY.
I MISS HER, TOO,

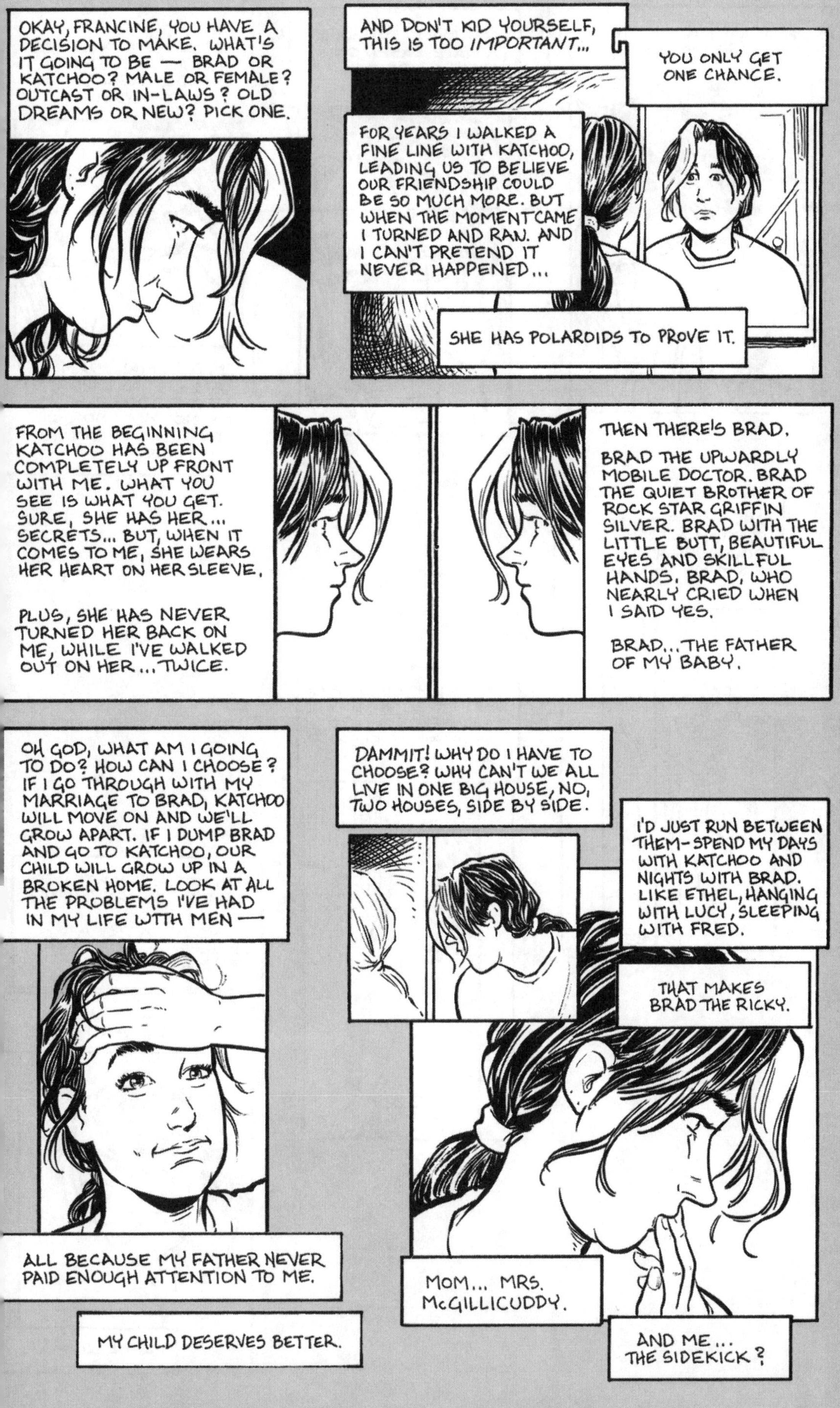
OKAY, FRANCINE, YOU HAVE A DECISION TO MAKE. WHAT'S IT GOING TO BE — BRAD OR KATCHOO? MALE OR FEMALE? OUTCAST OR IN-LAWS? OLD DREAMS OR NEW? PICK ONE.
AND DON'T KID YOURSELF, THIS IS TOO *IMPORTANT*...
YOU ONLY GET ONE CHANCE.
FOR YEARS I WALKED A FINE LINE WITH KATCHOO, LEADING US TO BELIEVE OUR FRIENDSHIP COULD BE SO MUCH MORE. BUT WHEN THE MOMENT CAME I TURNED AND RAN. AND I CAN'T PRETEND IT NEVER HAPPENED...
SHE HAS POLAROIDS TO PROVE IT.
FROM THE BEGINNING KATCHOO HAS BEEN COMPLETELY UP FRONT WITH ME. WHAT YOU SEE IS WHAT YOU GET. SURE, SHE HAS HER... SECRETS... BUT, WHEN IT COMES TO ME, SHE WEARS HER HEART ON HER SLEEVE.
PLUS, SHE HAS NEVER TURNED HER BACK ON ME, WHILE I'VE WALKED OUT ON HER... TWICE.
THEN THERE'S BRAD.
BRAD THE UPWARDLY MOBILE DOCTOR. BRAD THE QUIET BROTHER OF ROCK STAR GRIFFIN SILVER. BRAD WITH THE LITTLE BUTT, BEAUTIFUL EYES AND SKILLFUL HANDS. BRAD, WHO NEARLY CRIED WHEN I SAID YES.
BRAD... THE FATHER OF MY BABY.
OH GOD, WHAT AM I GOING TO DO? HOW CAN I CHOOSE? IF I GO THROUGH WITH MY MARRIAGE TO BRAD, KATCHOO WILL MOVE ON AND WE'LL GROW APART. IF I DUMP BRAD AND GO TO KATCHOO, OUR CHILD WILL GROW UP IN A BROKEN HOME. LOOK AT ALL THE PROBLEMS I'VE HAD IN MY LIFE WITH MEN —
ALL BECAUSE MY FATHER NEVER PAID ENOUGH ATTENTION TO ME.
MY CHILD DESERVES BETTER.
DAMMIT! WHY DO I HAVE TO CHOOSE? WHY CAN'T WE ALL LIVE IN ONE BIG HOUSE, NO, *TWO* HOUSES, SIDE BY SIDE.
I'D JUST RUN BETWEEN THEM — SPEND MY DAYS WITH KATCHOO AND NIGHTS WITH BRAD. LIKE ETHEL, HANGING WITH LUCY, SLEEPING WITH FRED.
THAT MAKES BRAD THE RICKY.
MOM... MRS. McGILLICUDDY.
AND ME... THE SIDEKICK?

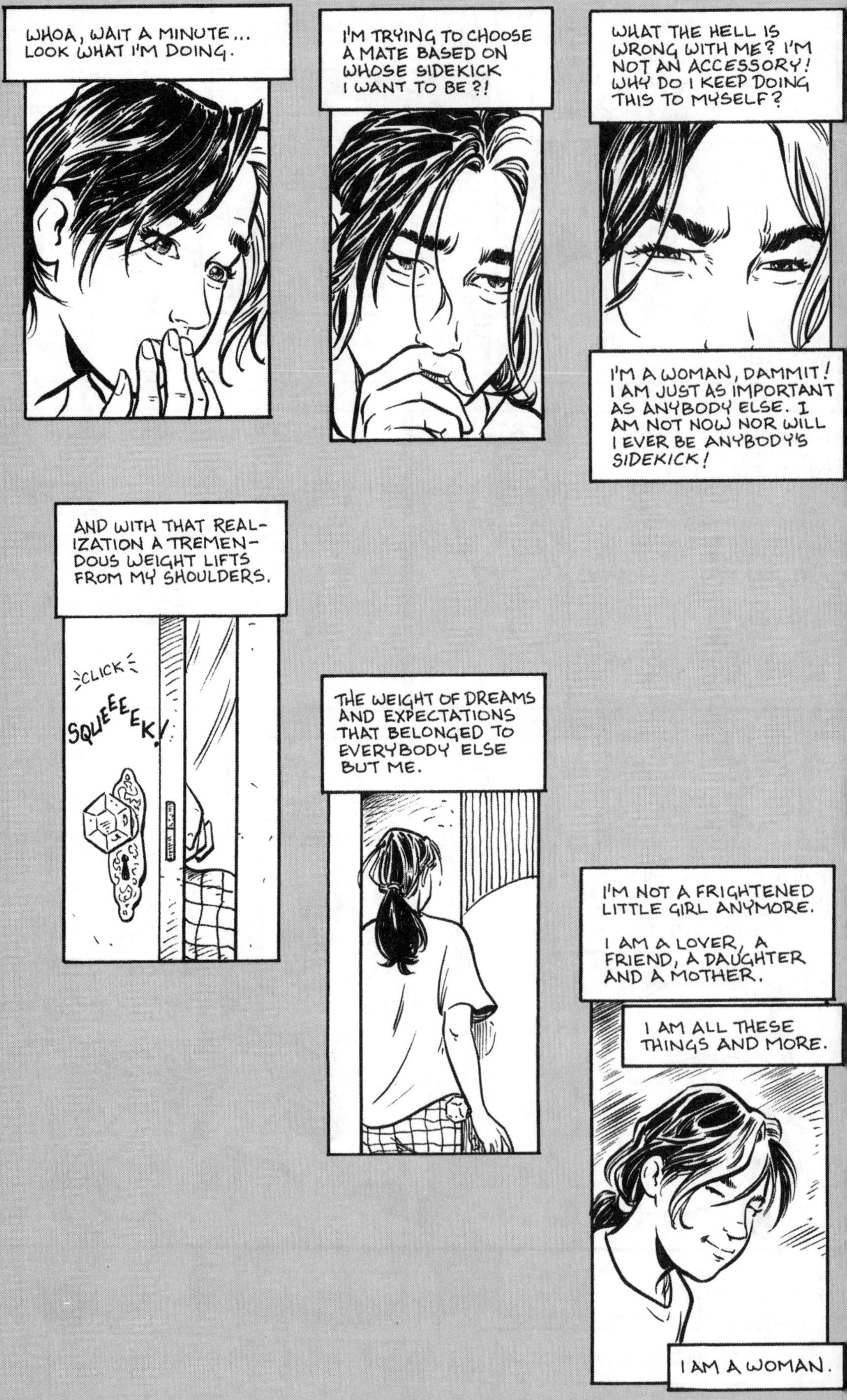
WHOA, WAIT A MINUTE... LOOK WHAT I'M DOING.
I'M TRYING TO CHOOSE A MATE BASED ON WHOSE SIDEKICK I WANT TO BE?!
WHAT THE HELL IS WRONG WITH ME? I'M NOT AN ACCESSORY! WHY DO I KEEP DOING THIS TO MYSELF?
I'M A WOMAN, DAMMIT! I AM JUST AS IMPORTANT AS ANYBODY ELSE. I AM NOT NOW NOR WILL I EVER BE ANYBODY'S SIDEKICK!
AND WITH THAT REALIZATION A TREMENDOUS WEIGHT LIFTS FROM MY SHOULDERS.
CLICK
SQUEEEEK!
THE WEIGHT OF DREAMS AND EXPECTATIONS THAT BELONGED TO EVERYBODY ELSE BUT ME.
I'M NOT A FRIGHTENED LITTLE GIRL ANYMORE.
I AM A LOVER, A FRIEND, A DAUGHTER AND A MOTHER.
I AM ALL THESE THINGS AND MORE.
I AM A WOMAN.

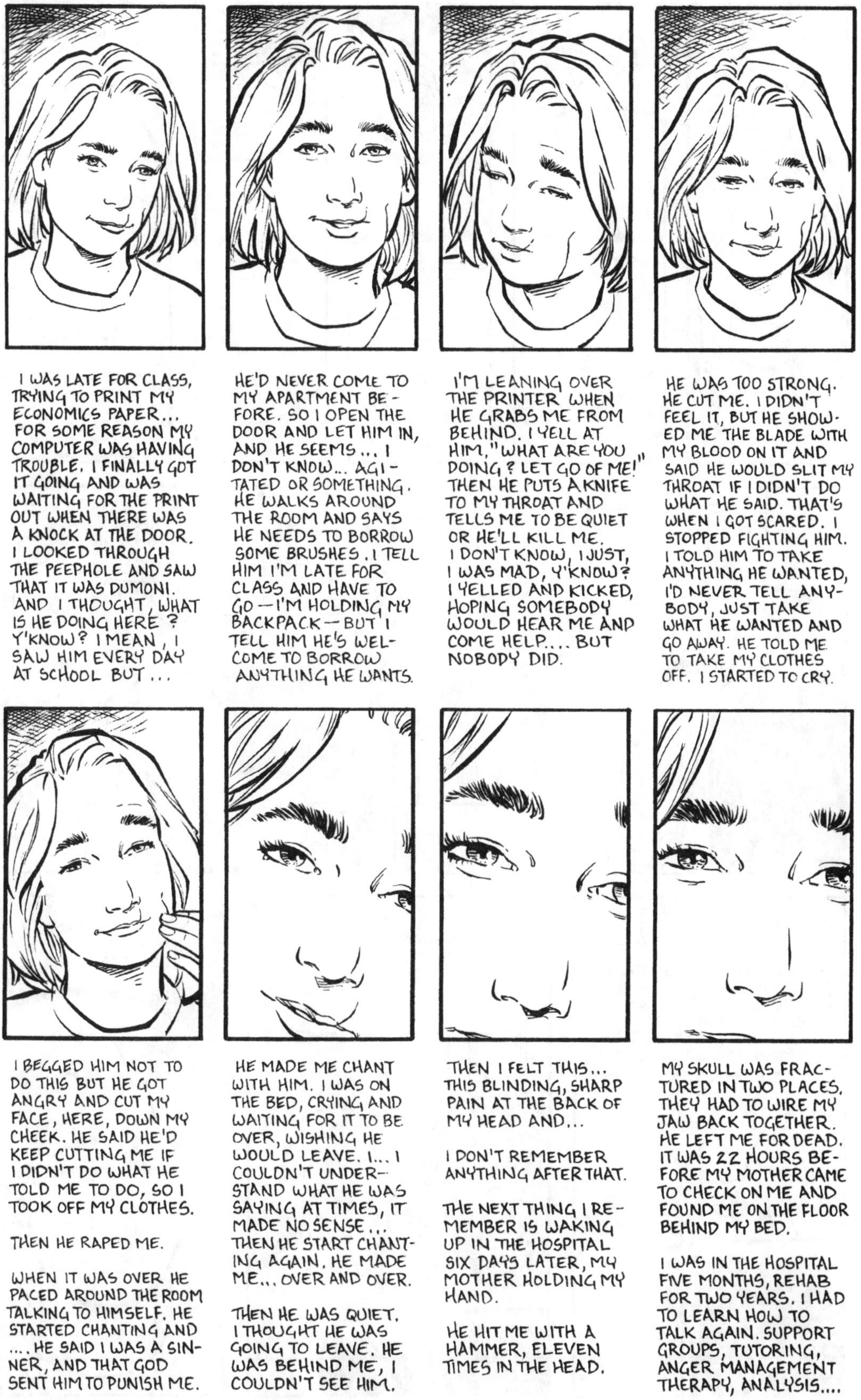
I WAS LATE FOR CLASS, TRYING TO PRINT MY ECONOMICS PAPER... FOR SOME REASON MY COMPUTER WAS HAVING TROUBLE. I FINALLY GOT IT GOING AND WAS WAITING FOR THE PRINT OUT WHEN THERE WAS A KNOCK AT THE DOOR. I LOOKED THROUGH THE PEEPHOLE AND SAW THAT IT WAS DUMONI. AND I THOUGHT, WHAT IS HE DOING HERE ? Y'KNOW? I MEAN, I SAW HIM EVERY DAY AT SCHOOL BUT...
HE'D NEVER COME TO MY APARTMENT BEFORE. SO I OPEN THE DOOR AND LET HIM IN, AND HE SEEMS... I DON'T KNOW... AGITATED OR SOMETHING. HE WALKS AROUND THE ROOM AND SAYS HE NEEDS TO BORROW SOME BRUSHES. I TELL HIM I'M LATE FOR CLASS AND HAVE TO GO—I'M HOLDING MY BACKPACK—BUT I TELL HIM HE'S WELCOME TO BORROW ANYTHING HE WANTS.
I'M LEANING OVER THE PRINTER WHEN HE GRABS ME FROM BEHIND. I YELL AT HIM, "WHAT ARE YOU DOING? LET GO OF ME!" THEN HE PUTS A KNIFE TO MY THROAT AND TELLS ME TO BE QUIET OR HE'LL KILL ME. I DON'T KNOW, I JUST, I WAS MAD, Y'KNOW? I YELLED AND KICKED, HOPING SOMEBODY WOULD HEAR ME AND COME HELP.... BUT NOBODY DID.
HE WAS TOO STRONG. HE CUT ME. I DIDN'T FEEL IT, BUT HE SHOWED ME THE BLADE WITH MY BLOOD ON IT AND SAID HE WOULD SLIT MY THROAT IF I DIDN'T DO WHAT HE SAID. THAT'S WHEN I GOT SCARED. I STOPPED FIGHTING HIM. I TOLD HIM TO TAKE ANYTHING HE WANTED, I'D NEVER TELL ANYBODY, JUST TAKE WHAT HE WANTED AND GO AWAY. HE TOLD ME TO TAKE MY CLOTHES OFF. I STARTED TO CRY.
I BEGGED HIM NOT TO DO THIS BUT HE GOT ANGRY AND CUT MY FACE, HERE, DOWN MY CHEEK. HE SAID HE'D KEEP CUTTING ME IF I DIDN'T DO WHAT HE TOLD ME TO DO, SO I TOOK OFF MY CLOTHES.
THEN HE RAPED ME.
WHEN IT WAS OVER HE PACED AROUND THE ROOM TALKING TO HIMSELF. HE STARTED CHANTING AND .... HE SAID I WAS A SINNER, AND THAT GOD SENT HIM TO PUNISH ME.
HE MADE ME CHANT WITH HIM. I WAS ON THE BED, CRYING AND WAITING FOR IT TO BE OVER, WISHING HE WOULD LEAVE. I... I COULDN'T UNDERSTAND WHAT HE WAS SAYING AT TIMES, IT MADE NO SENSE... THEN HE START CHANTING AGAIN. HE MADE ME... OVER AND OVER.
THEN HE WAS QUIET. I THOUGHT HE WAS GOING TO LEAVE. HE WAS BEHIND ME, I COULDN'T SEE HIM.
THEN I FELT THIS... THIS BLINDING, SHARP PAIN AT THE BACK OF MY HEAD AND...
I DON'T REMEMBER ANYTHING AFTER THAT.
THE NEXT THING I REMEMBER IS WAKING UP IN THE HOSPITAL SIX DAYS LATER, MY MOTHER HOLDING MY HAND.
HE HIT ME WITH A HAMMER, ELEVEN TIMES IN THE HEAD.
MY SKULL WAS FRACTURED IN TWO PLACES. THEY HAD TO WIRE MY JAW BACK TOGETHER. HE LEFT ME FOR DEAD. IT WAS 22 HOURS BEFORE MY MOTHER CAME TO CHECK ON ME AND FOUND ME ON THE FLOOR BEHIND MY BED.
I WAS IN THE HOSPITAL FIVE MONTHS, REHAB FOR TWO YEARS. I HAD TO LEARN HOW TO TALK AGAIN. SUPPORT GROUPS, TUTORING, ANGER MANAGEMENT THERAPY, ANALYSIS....

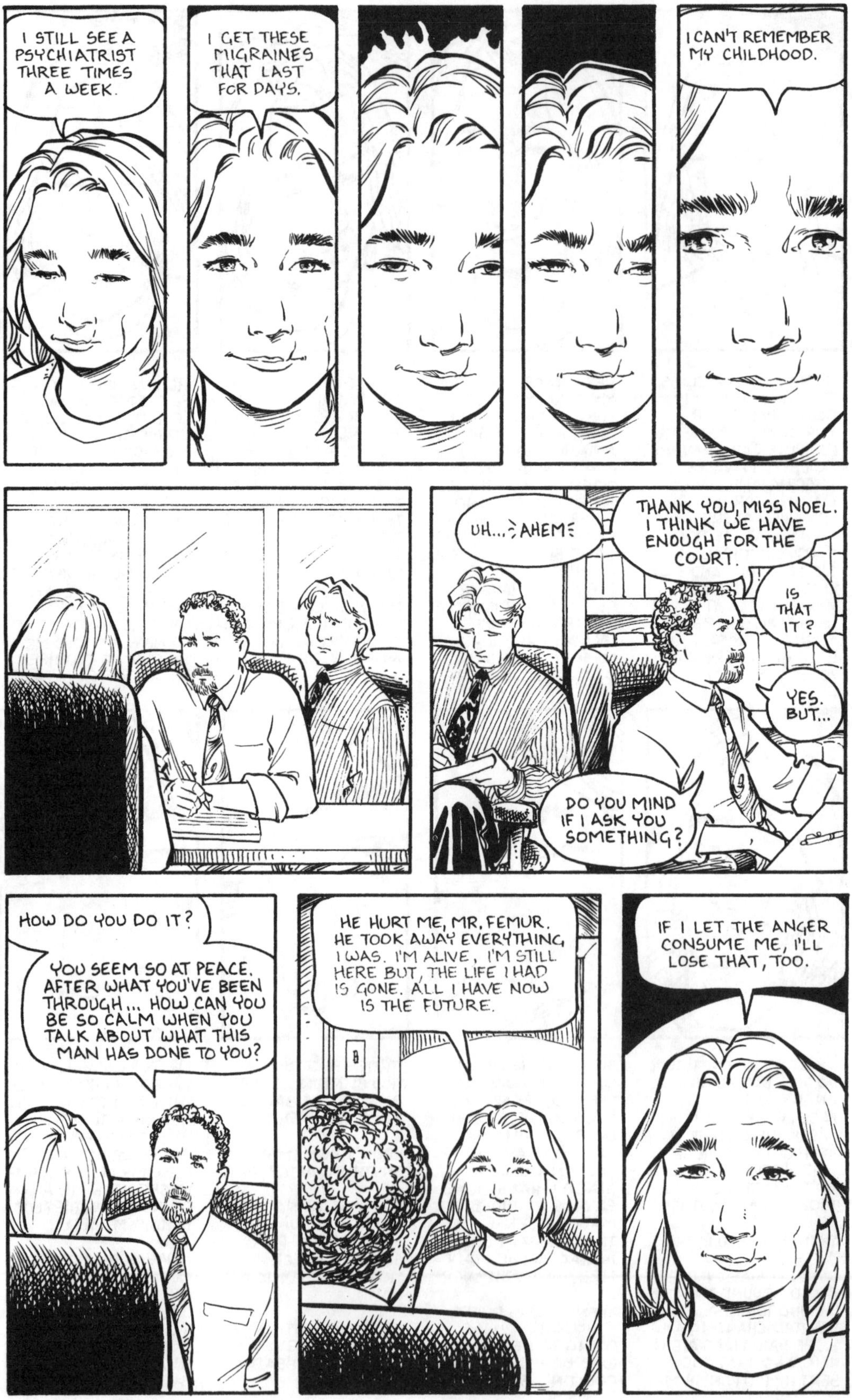
I STILL SEE A PSYCHIATRIST THREE TIMES A WEEK.
I GET THESE MIGRAINES THAT LAST FOR DAYS.
I CAN'T REMEMBER MY CHILDHOOD.
UH... AHEM
THANK YOU, MISS NOEL. I THINK WE HAVE ENOUGH FOR THE COURT.
IS THAT IT?
YES. BUT...
DO YOU MIND IF I ASK YOU SOMETHING?
HOW DO YOU DO IT?
YOU SEEM SO AT PEACE. AFTER WHAT YOU'VE BEEN THROUGH... HOW CAN YOU BE SO CALM WHEN YOU TALK ABOUT WHAT THIS MAN HAS DONE TO YOU?
HE HURT ME, MR. FEMUR. HE TOOK AWAY EVERYTHING I WAS. I'M ALIVE, I'M STILL HERE BUT, THE LIFE I HAD IS GONE. ALL I HAVE NOW IS THE FUTURE.
IF I LET THE ANGER CONSUME ME, I'LL LOSE THAT, TOO.

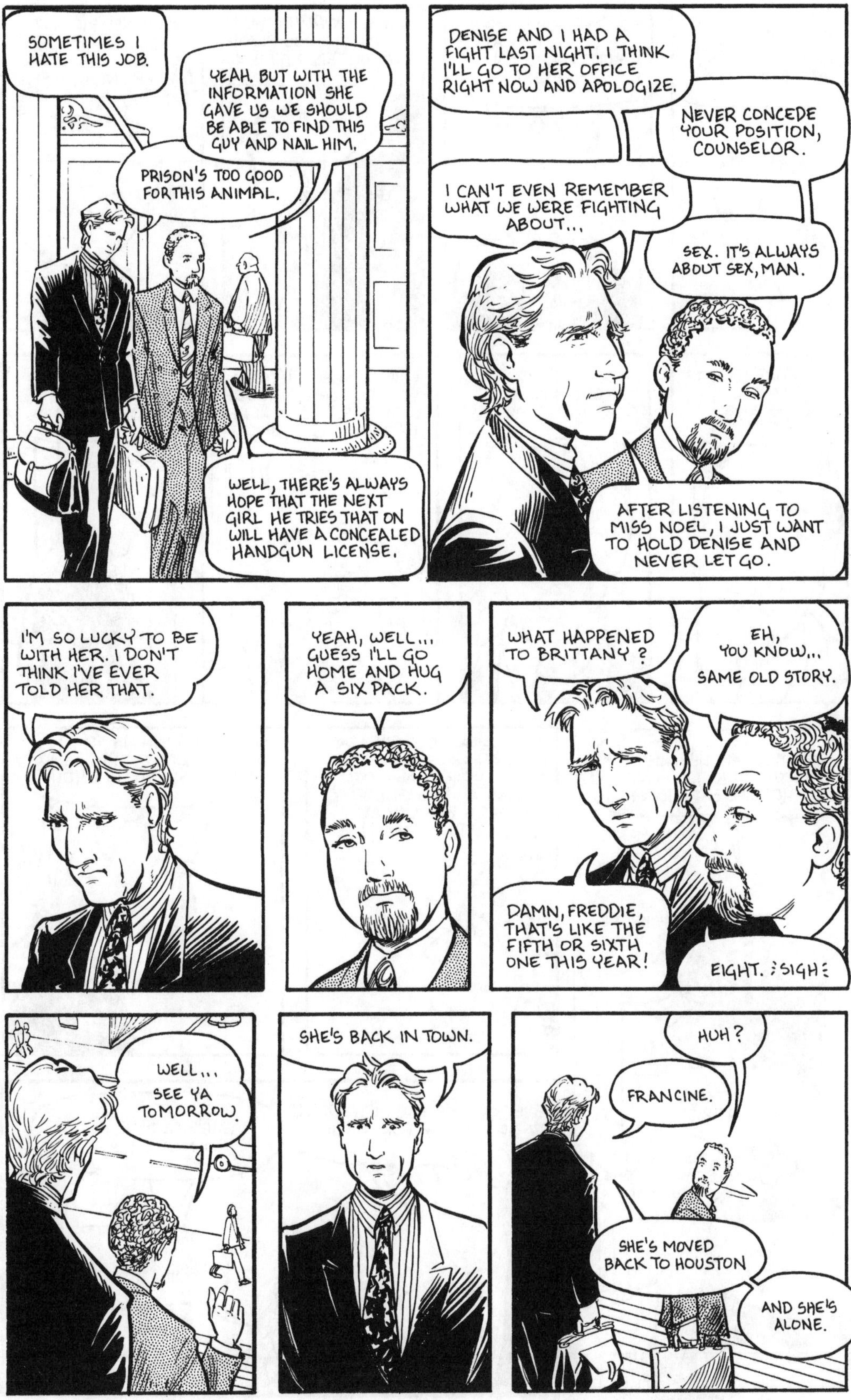
SOMETIMES I HATE THIS JOB.
YEAH. BUT WITH THE INFORMATION SHE GAVE US WE SHOULD BE ABLE TO FIND THIS GUY AND NAIL HIM.
PRISON'S TOO GOOD FOR THIS ANIMAL.
WELL, THERE'S ALWAYS HOPE THAT THE NEXT GIRL HE TRIES THAT ON WILL HAVE A CONCEALED HANDGUN LICENSE.
DENISE AND I HAD A FIGHT LAST NIGHT. I THINK I'LL GO TO HER OFFICE RIGHT NOW AND APOLOGIZE.
NEVER CONCEDE YOUR POSITION, COUNSELOR.
I CAN'T EVEN REMEMBER WHAT WE WERE FIGHTING ABOUT...
SEX. IT'S ALWAYS ABOUT SEX, MAN.
AFTER LISTENING TO MISS NOEL, I JUST WANT TO HOLD DENISE AND NEVER LET GO.
I'M SO LUCKY TO BE WITH HER. I DON'T THINK I'VE EVER TOLD HER THAT.
YEAH, WELL... GUESS I'LL GO HOME AND HUG A SIX PACK.
WHAT HAPPENED TO BRITTANY?
EH, YOU KNOW... SAME OLD STORY.
DAMN, FREDDIE, THAT'S LIKE THE FIFTH OR SIXTH ONE THIS YEAR!
EIGHT. :SIGH:
WELL... SEE YA TOMORROW.
SHE'S BACK IN TOWN.
HUH?
FRANCINE.
SHE'S MOVED BACK TO HOUSTON
AND SHE'S ALONE.

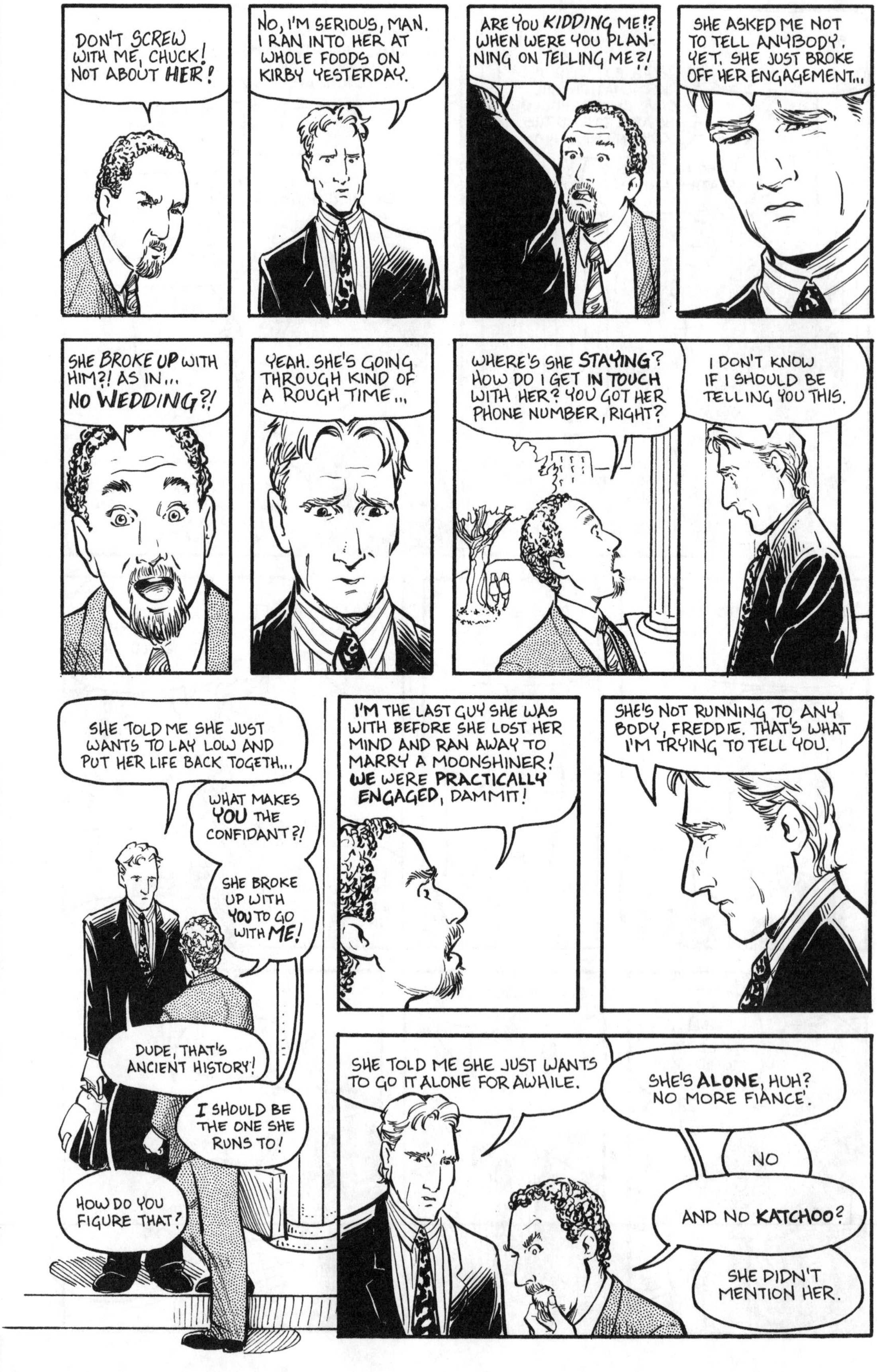

DON'T SCREW WITH ME, CHUCK! NOT ABOUT HER!
NO, I'M SERIOUS, MAN. I RAN INTO HER AT WHOLE FOODS ON KIRBY YESTERDAY.
ARE YOU KIDDING ME!? WHEN WERE YOU PLANNING ON TELLING ME?!
SHE ASKED ME NOT TO TELL ANYBODY. YET. SHE JUST BROKE OFF HER ENGAGEMENT...
SHE BROKE UP WITH HIM?! AS IN... NO WEDDING?!
YEAH. SHE'S GOING THROUGH KIND OF A ROUGH TIME...
WHERE'S SHE STAYING? HOW DO I GET IN TOUCH WITH HER? YOU GOT HER PHONE NUMBER, RIGHT?
I DON'T KNOW IF I SHOULD BE TELLING YOU THIS.
SHE TOLD ME SHE JUST WANTS TO LAY LOW AND PUT HER LIFE BACK TOGETH...
WHAT MAKES YOU THE CONFIDANT?!
SHE BROKE UP WITH YOU TO GO WITH ME!
DUDE, THAT'S ANCIENT HISTORY!
I SHOULD BE THE ONE SHE RUNS TO!
HOW DO YOU FIGURE THAT?
I'M THE LAST GUY SHE WAS WITH BEFORE SHE LOST HER MIND AND RAN AWAY TO MARRY A MOONSHINER! WE WERE PRACTICALLY ENGAGED, DAMMIT!
SHE'S NOT RUNNING TO ANY BODY, FREDDIE. THAT'S WHAT I'M TRYING TO TELL YOU.
SHE TOLD ME SHE JUST WANTS TO GO IT ALONE FOR AWHILE.
SHE'S ALONE, HUH? NO MORE FIANCE'.
NO
AND NO KATCHOO?
SHE DIDN'T MENTION HER.

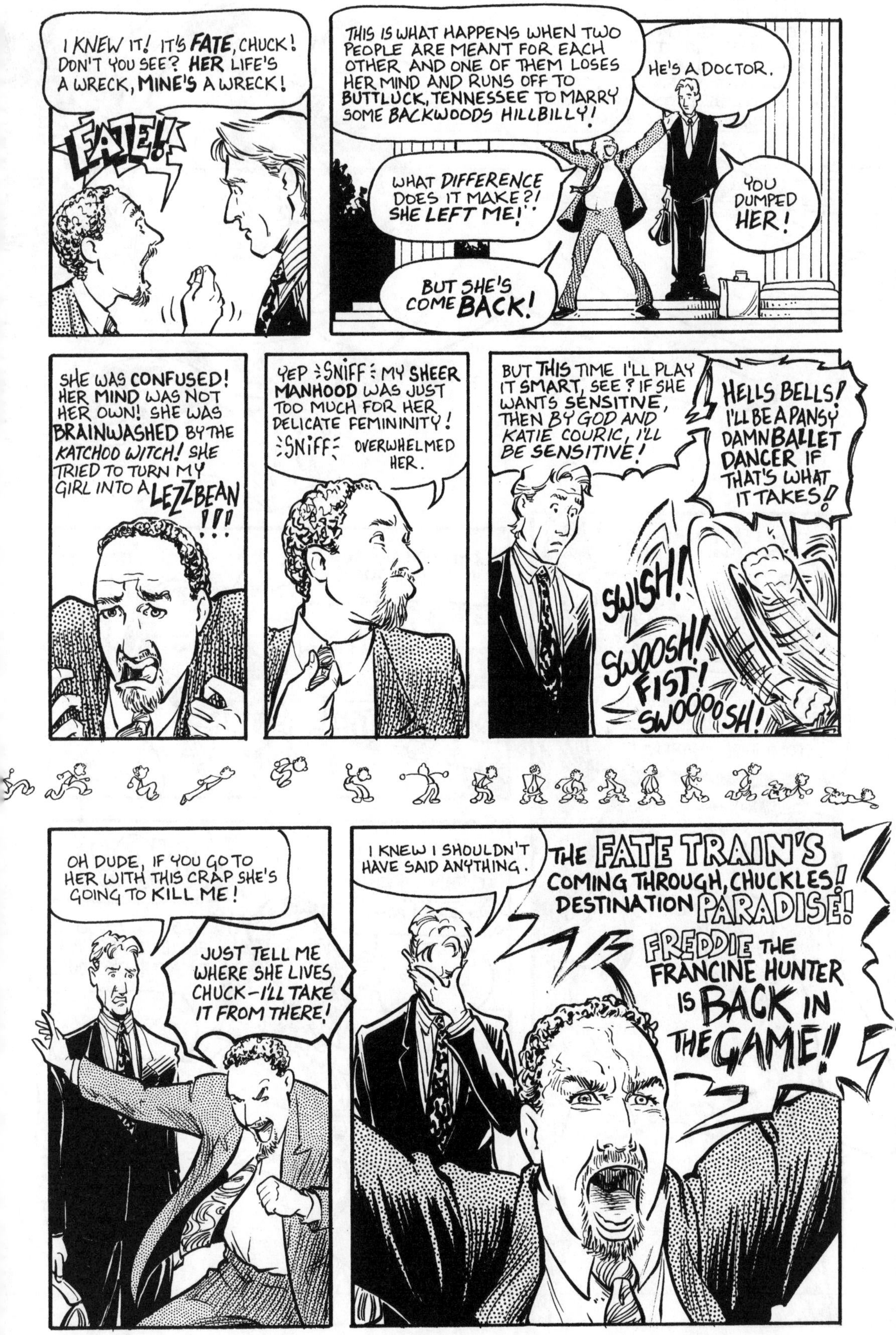

I KNEW IT! IT'S FATE, CHUCK! DON'T YOU SEE? HER LIFE'S A WRECK, MINE'S A WRECK!
FATE!
THIS IS WHAT HAPPENS WHEN TWO PEOPLE ARE MEANT FOR EACH OTHER AND ONE OF THEM LOSES HER MIND AND RUNS OFF TO BUTTLUCK, TENNESSEE TO MARRY SOME BACKWOODS HILLBILLY!
HE'S A DOCTOR.
WHAT DIFFERENCE DOES IT MAKE?! SHE LEFT ME!
YOU DUMPED HER!
BUT SHE'S COME BACK!
SHE WAS CONFUSED! HER MIND WAS NOT HER OWN! SHE WAS BRAINWASHED BY THE KATCHOO WITCH! SHE TRIED TO TURN MY GIRL INTO A LEZZBEAN!!!
YEP SNIFF MY SHEER MANHOOD WAS JUST TOO MUCH FOR HER DELICATE FEMININITY! SNIFF OVERWHELMED HER.
BUT THIS TIME I'LL PLAY IT SMART, SEE? IF SHE WANTS SENSITIVE, THEN BY GOD AND KATIE COURIC, I'LL BE SENSITIVE!
HELLS BELLS! I'LL BE A PANSY DAMN BALLET DANCER IF THAT'S WHAT IT TAKES!
SWISH! SWOOSH! FIST! SWOOOOSH!
OH DUDE, IF YOU GO TO HER WITH THIS CRAP SHE'S GOING TO KILL ME!
JUST TELL ME WHERE SHE LIVES, CHUCK—I'LL TAKE IT FROM THERE!
I KNEW I SHOULDN'T HAVE SAID ANYTHING.
THE FATE TRAIN'S COMING THROUGH, CHUCKLES! DESTINATION PARADISE!
FREDDIE THE FRANCINE HUNTER IS BACK IN THE GAME!!

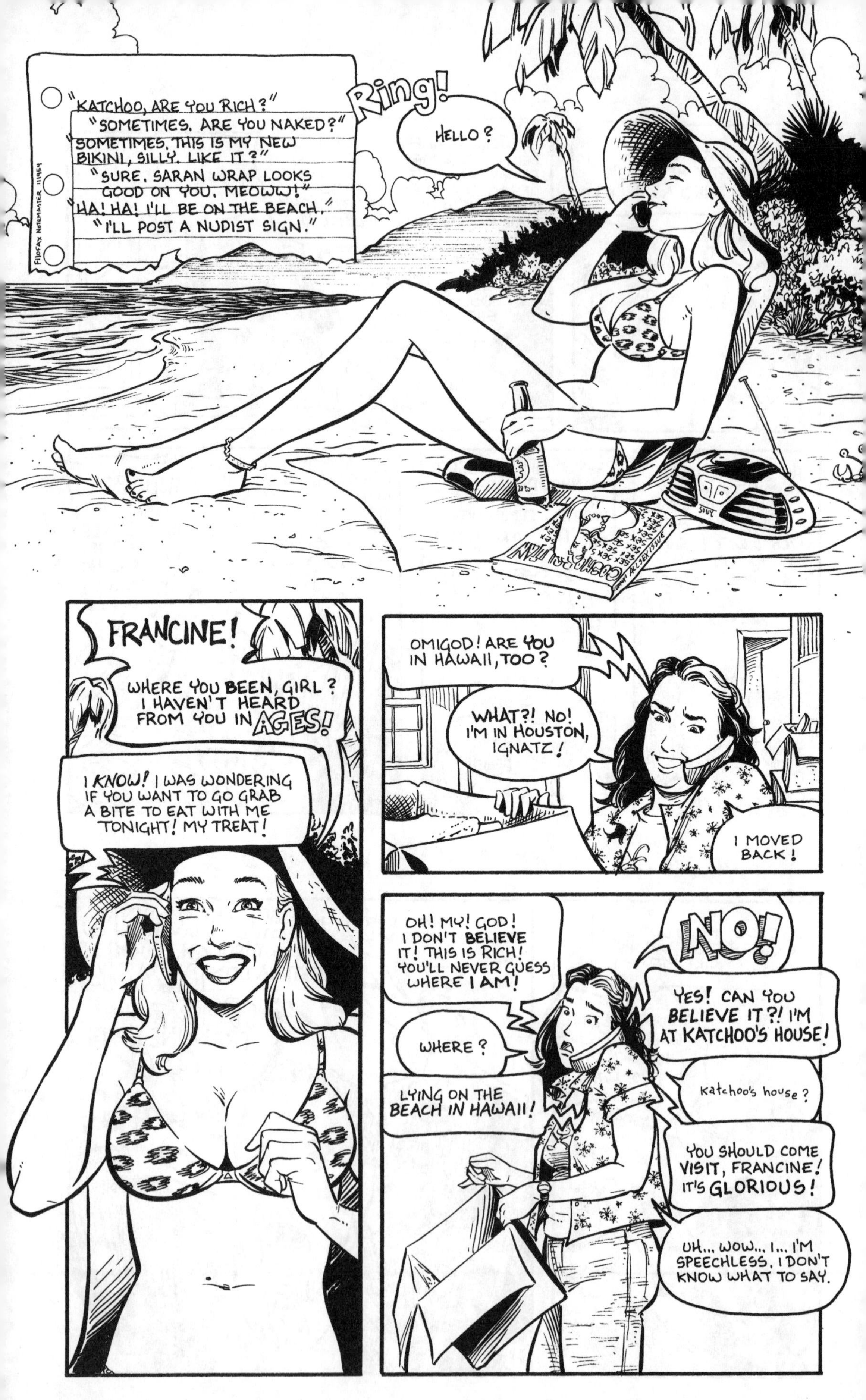

"KATCHOO, ARE YOU RICH?"
"SOMETIMES. ARE YOU NAKED?"
"SOMETIMES. THIS IS MY NEW BIKINI, SILLY. LIKE IT?"
"SURE. SARAN WRAP LOOKS GOOD ON YOU. MEOWW!"
"HA! HA! I'LL BE ON THE BEACH."
"I'LL POST A NUDIST SIGN."
Ring!
HELLO?
FRANCINE!
WHERE YOU BEEN, GIRL? I HAVEN'T HEARD FROM YOU IN AGES!
I KNOW! I WAS WONDERING IF YOU WANT TO GO GRAB A BITE TO EAT WITH ME TONIGHT! MY TREAT!
OMIGOD! ARE YOU IN HAWAII, TOO?
WHAT?! NO! I'M IN HOUSTON, IGNATZ!
I MOVED BACK!
OH! MY! GOD! I DON'T BELIEVE IT! THIS IS RICH! YOU'LL NEVER GUESS WHERE I AM!
WHERE?
LYING ON THE BEACH IN HAWAII!
NO!
YES! CAN YOU BELIEVE IT?! I'M AT KATCHOO'S HOUSE!
Katchoo's house?
YOU SHOULD COME VISIT, FRANCINE! IT'S GLORIOUS!
UH... WOW... I... I'M SPEECHLESS, I DON'T KNOW WHAT TO SAY.

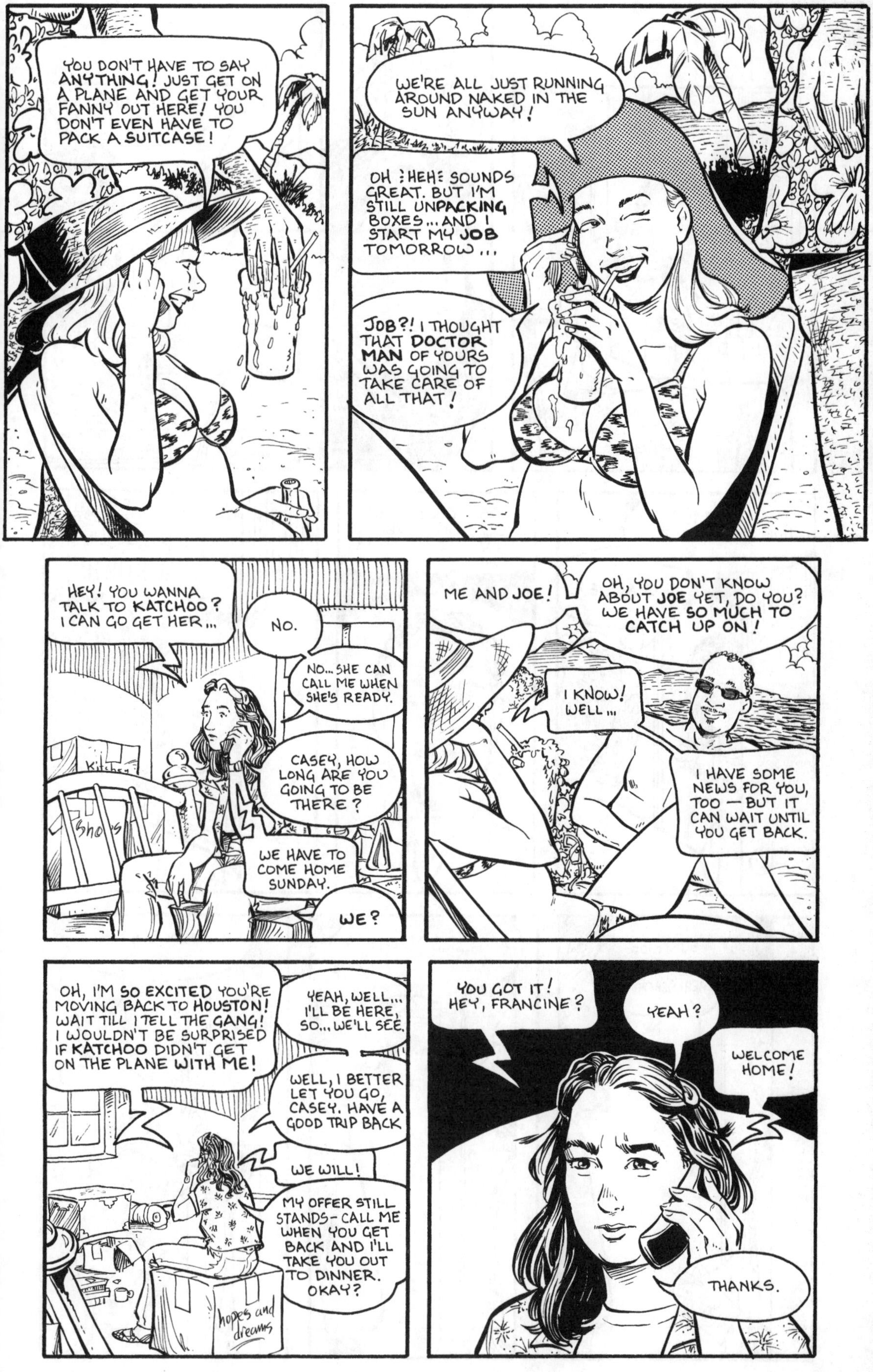
YOU DON'T HAVE TO SAY ANYTHING! JUST GET ON A PLANE AND GET YOUR FANNY OUT HERE! YOU DON'T EVEN HAVE TO PACK A SUITCASE!
WE'RE ALL JUST RUNNING AROUND NAKED IN THE SUN ANYWAY!
OH ⁝HEH⁝ SOUNDS GREAT. BUT I'M STILL UNPACKING BOXES... AND I START MY JOB TOMORROW...
JOB?! I THOUGHT THAT DOCTOR MAN OF YOURS WAS GOING TO TAKE CARE OF ALL THAT!
HEY! YOU WANNA TALK TO KATCHOO? I CAN GO GET HER...
NO.
NO... SHE CAN CALL ME WHEN SHE'S READY.
CASEY, HOW LONG ARE YOU GOING TO BE THERE?
WE HAVE TO COME HOME SUNDAY.
WE?
Kitchen
Shoes
ME AND JOE!
OH, YOU DON'T KNOW ABOUT JOE YET, DO YOU? WE HAVE SO MUCH TO CATCH UP ON!
I KNOW! WELL...
I HAVE SOME NEWS FOR YOU, TOO — BUT IT CAN WAIT UNTIL YOU GET BACK.
OH, I'M SO EXCITED YOU'RE MOVING BACK TO HOUSTON! WAIT TILL I TELL THE GANG! I WOULDN'T BE SURPRISED IF KATCHOO DIDN'T GET ON THE PLANE WITH ME!
YEAH, WELL... I'LL BE HERE, SO... WE'LL SEE.
WELL, I BETTER LET YOU GO, CASEY. HAVE A GOOD TRIP BACK.
WE WILL!
MY OFFER STILL STANDS- CALL ME WHEN YOU GET BACK AND I'LL TAKE YOU OUT TO DINNER. OKAY?
hopes and dreams
YOU GOT IT! HEY, FRANCINE?
YEAH?
WELCOME HOME!
THANKS.

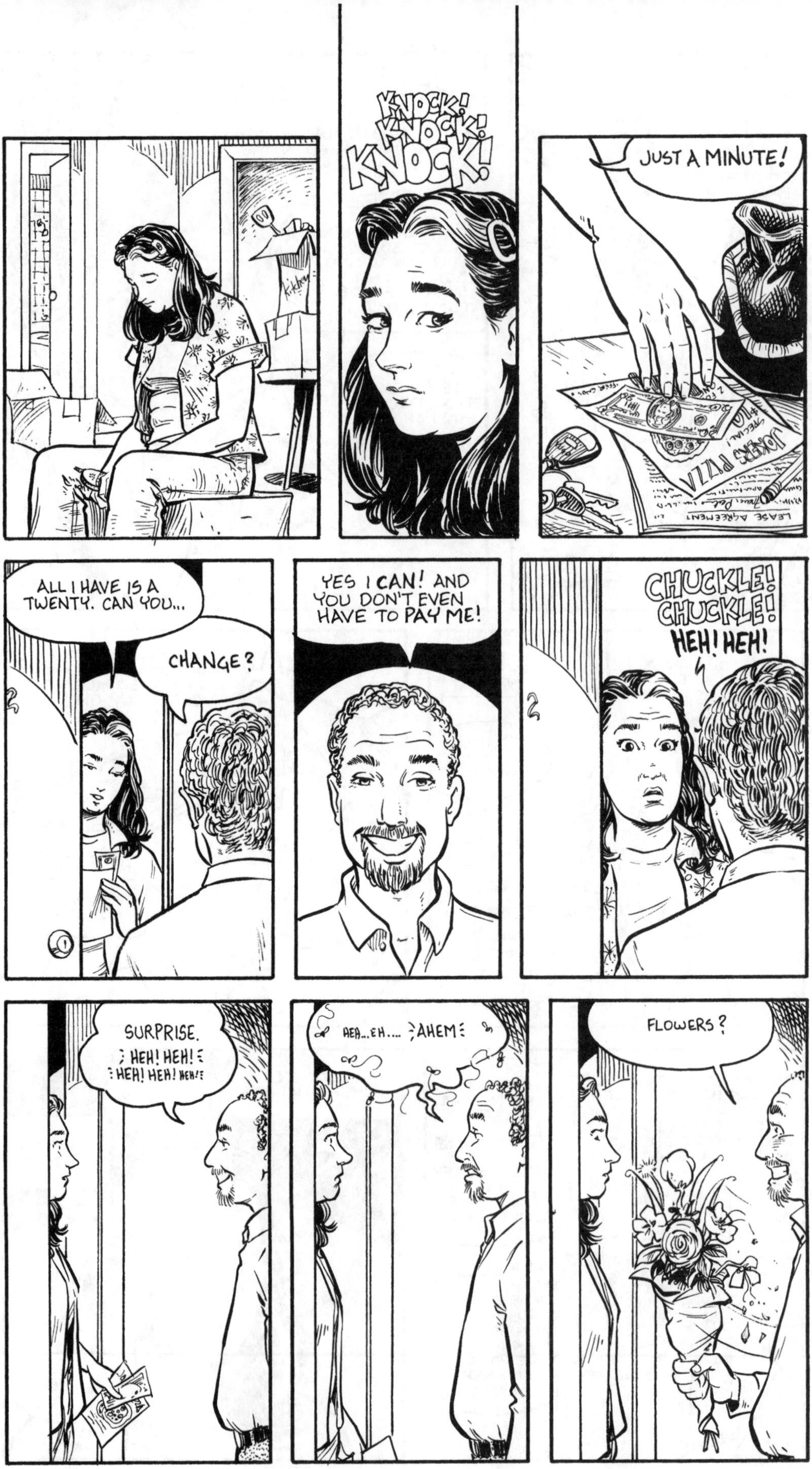
KNOCK! KNOCK! KNOCK!
JUST A MINUTE!
ALL I HAVE IS A TWENTY. CAN YOU...
CHANGE?
YES I CAN! AND YOU DON'T EVEN HAVE TO PAY ME!
CHUCKLE! CHUCKLE! HEH! HEH!
SURPRISE.
HEH! HEH! HEH! HEH! HEH!
HEH...EH.... AHEM
FLOWERS?

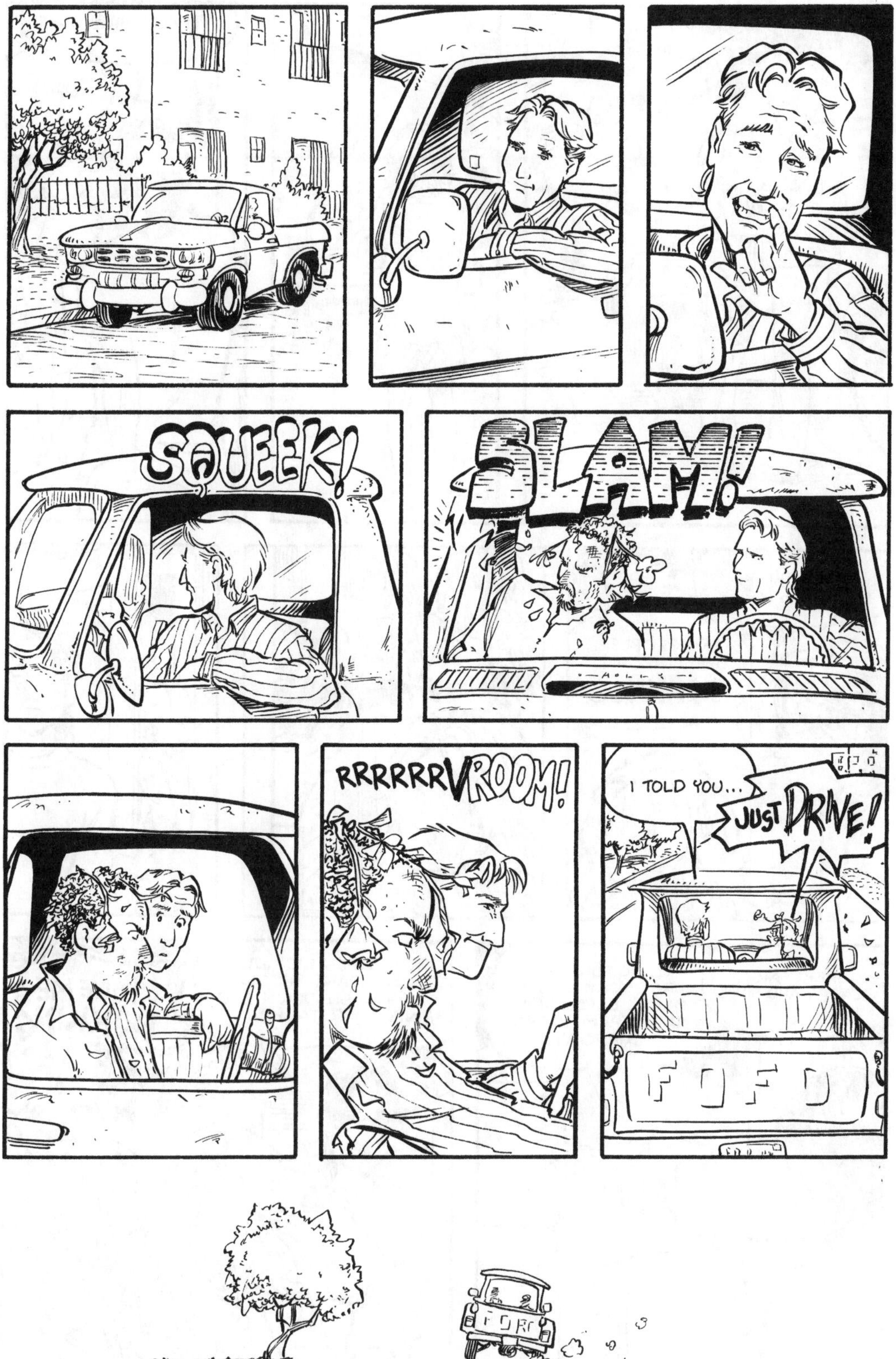
SQUEEK!
SLAM!
RRRRRRVROOM!
I TOLD YOU...
JUST DRIVE!

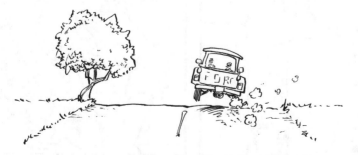

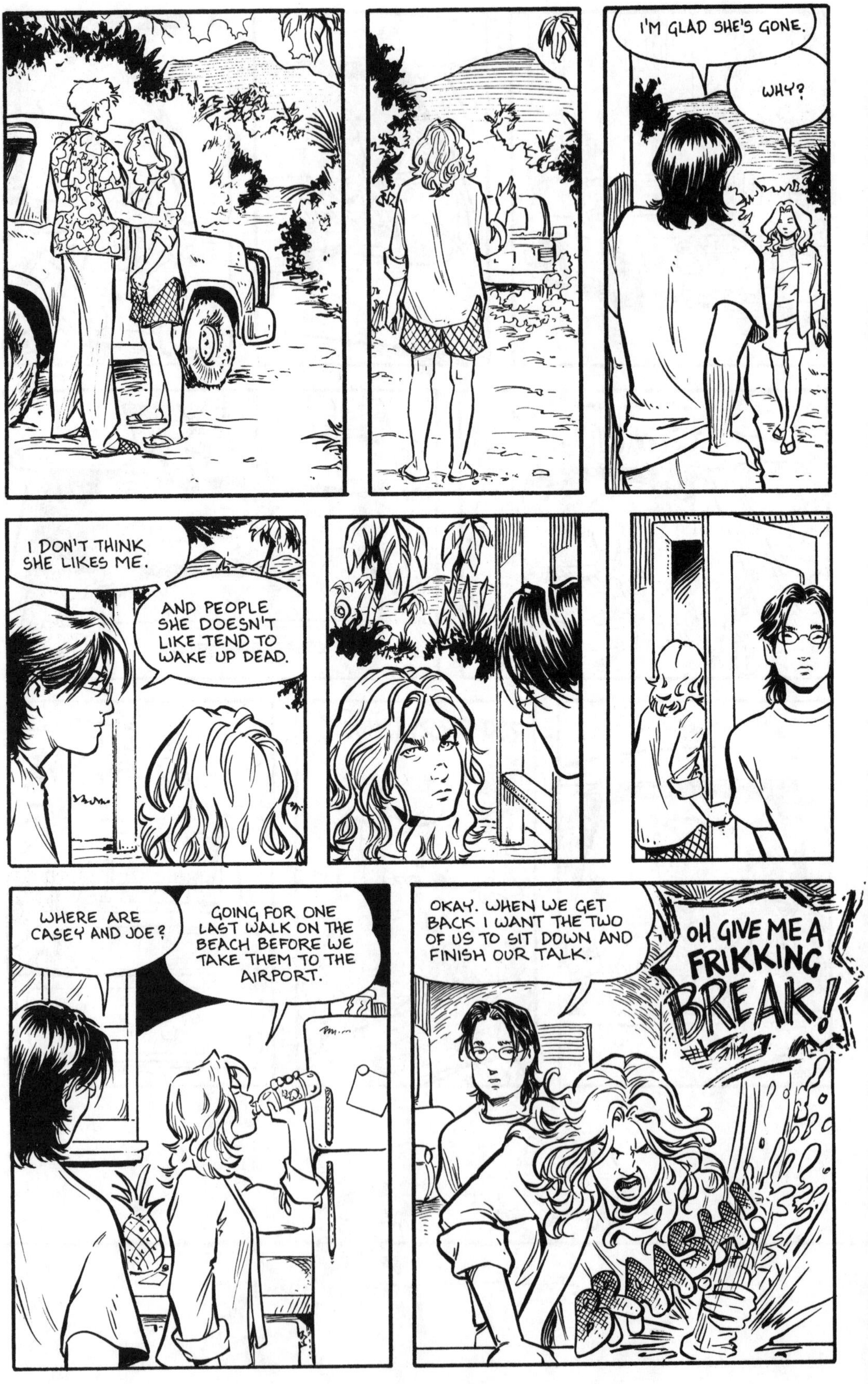

I'M GLAD SHE'S GONE.
WHY?
I DON'T THINK SHE LIKES ME.
AND PEOPLE SHE DOESN'T LIKE TEND TO WAKE UP DEAD.
WHERE ARE CASEY AND JOE?
GOING FOR ONE LAST WALK ON THE BEACH BEFORE WE TAKE THEM TO THE AIRPORT.
OKAY. WHEN WE GET BACK I WANT THE TWO OF US TO SIT DOWN AND FINISH OUR TALK.
OH GIVE ME A FRIKKING BREAK!

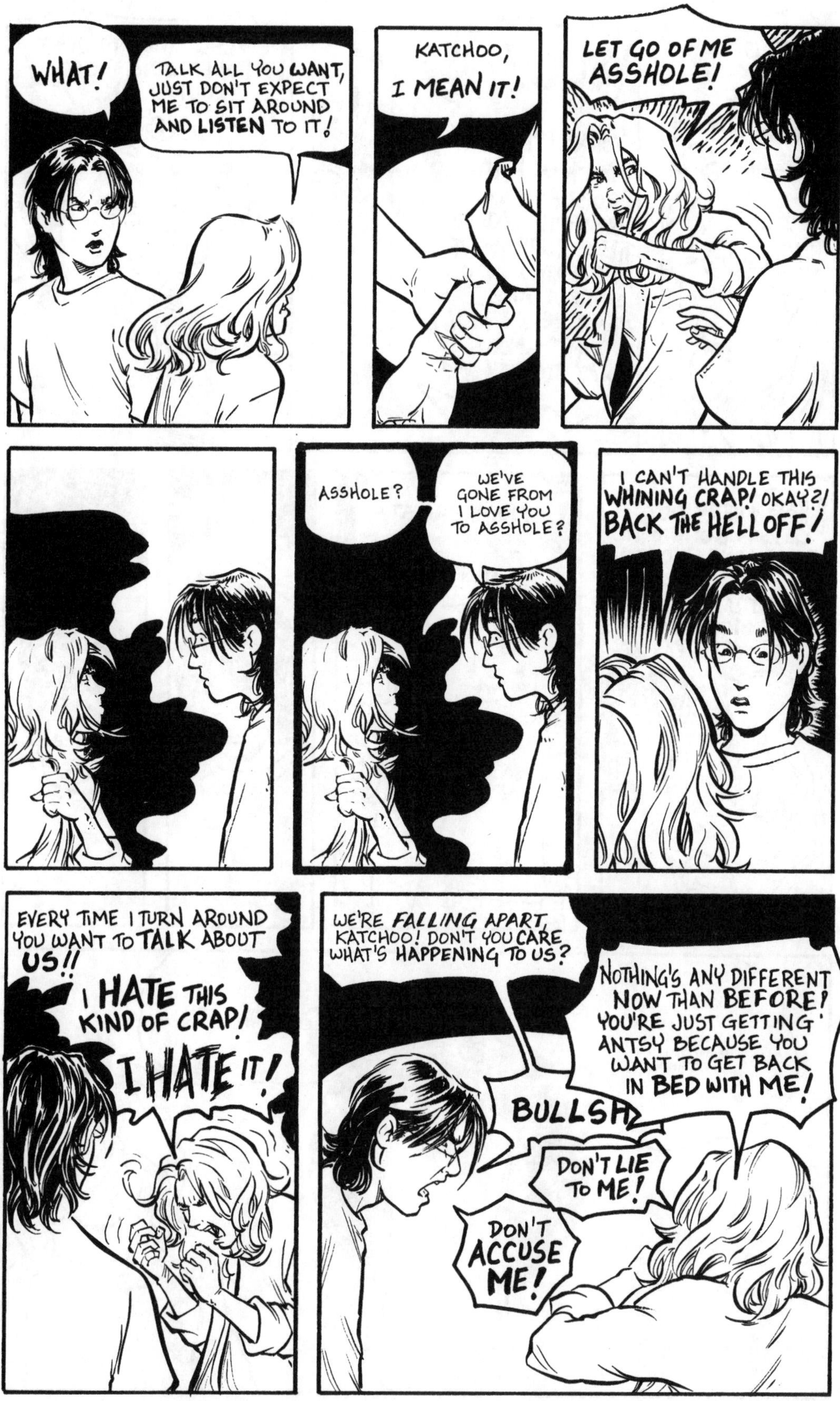
WHAT!
TALK ALL YOU WANT, JUST DON'T EXPECT ME TO SIT AROUND AND LISTEN TO IT!
KATCHOO, I MEAN IT!
LET GO OF ME ASSHOLE!
ASSHOLE?
WE'VE GONE FROM I LOVE YOU TO ASSHOLE?
I CAN'T HANDLE THIS WHINING CRAP! OKAY?! BACK THE HELL OFF!
EVERY TIME I TURN AROUND YOU WANT TO TALK ABOUT US!!
I HATE THIS KIND OF CRAP!
I HATE IT!
WE'RE FALLING APART, KATCHOO! DON'T YOU CARE WHAT'S HAPPENING TO US?
NOTHING'S ANY DIFFERENT NOW THAN BEFORE! YOU'RE JUST GETTING ANTSY BECAUSE YOU WANT TO GET BACK IN BED WITH ME!
BULLSH
DON'T LIE TO ME!
DON'T ACCUSE ME!

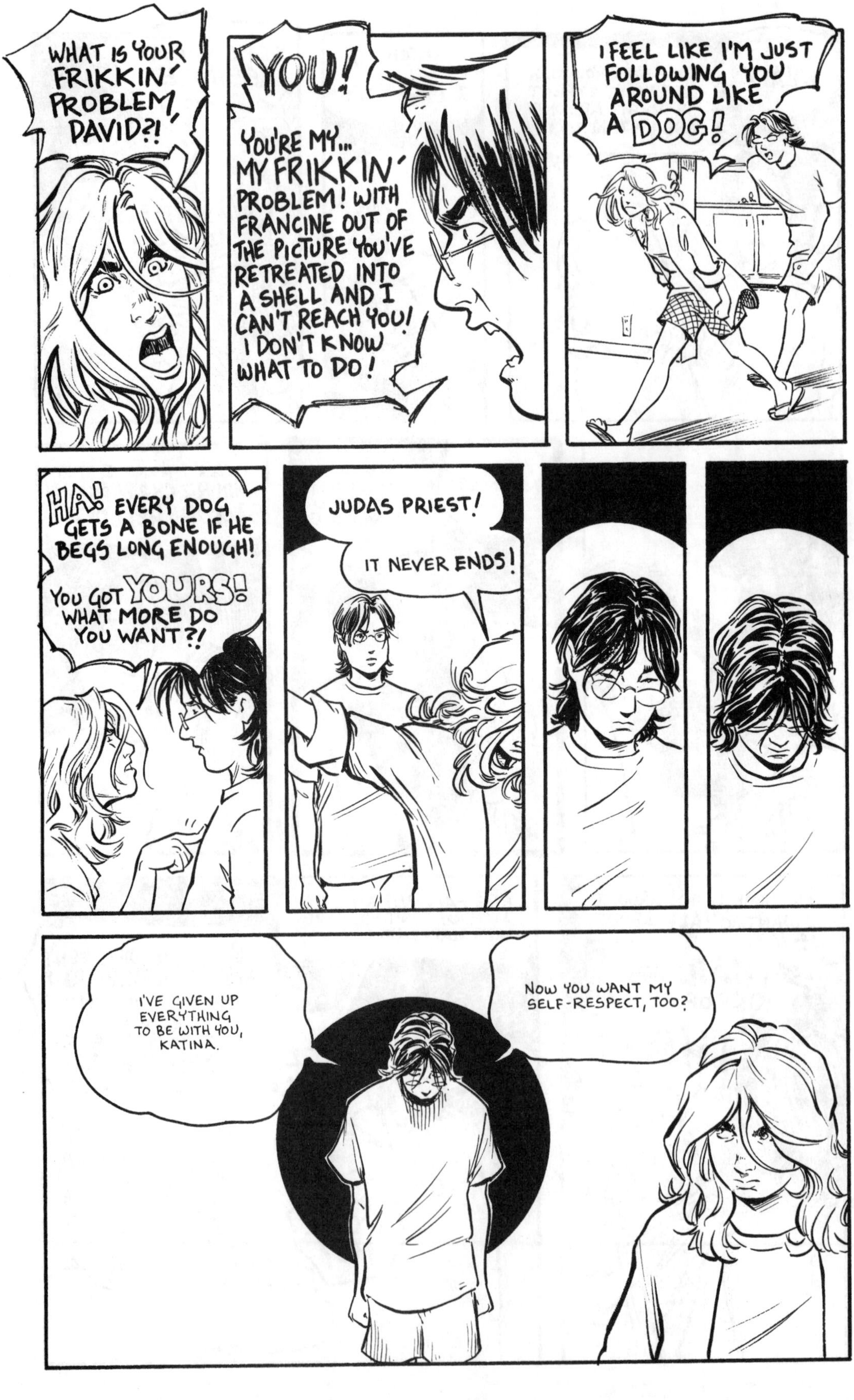
WHAT IS YOUR FRIKKIN' PROBLEM, DAVID?!
YOU!
YOU'RE MY... MY FRIKKIN' PROBLEM! WITH FRANCINE OUT OF THE PICTURE YOU'VE RETREATED INTO A SHELL AND I CAN'T REACH YOU! I DON'T KNOW WHAT TO DO!
I FEEL LIKE I'M JUST FOLLOWING YOU AROUND LIKE A DOG!
HA! EVERY DOG GETS A BONE IF HE BEGS LONG ENOUGH!
YOU GOT YOURS! WHAT MORE DO YOU WANT?!
JUDAS PRIEST!
IT NEVER ENDS!
I'VE GIVEN UP EVERYTHING TO BE WITH YOU, KATINA.
NOW YOU WANT MY SELF-RESPECT, TOO?

HONK!

COME ON GUYS! LET'S GO!

HONK!

HONK!

WE... WE NEED TO GO.

DAVID?

DAVID?

HO HONK!

YOO HOO!

WHERE'S DAVID? ISN'T HE COMING?

NO.

BUT I DIDN'T GET TO SAY GOODBYE.

FORGET IT. WE'D BETTER ROLL IF YOU'RE GOING TO MAKE YOUR PLANE.

RRRRR... VROOOM! RRRRRR

RRRRR....

GGRRRRR

RRAAAGH!

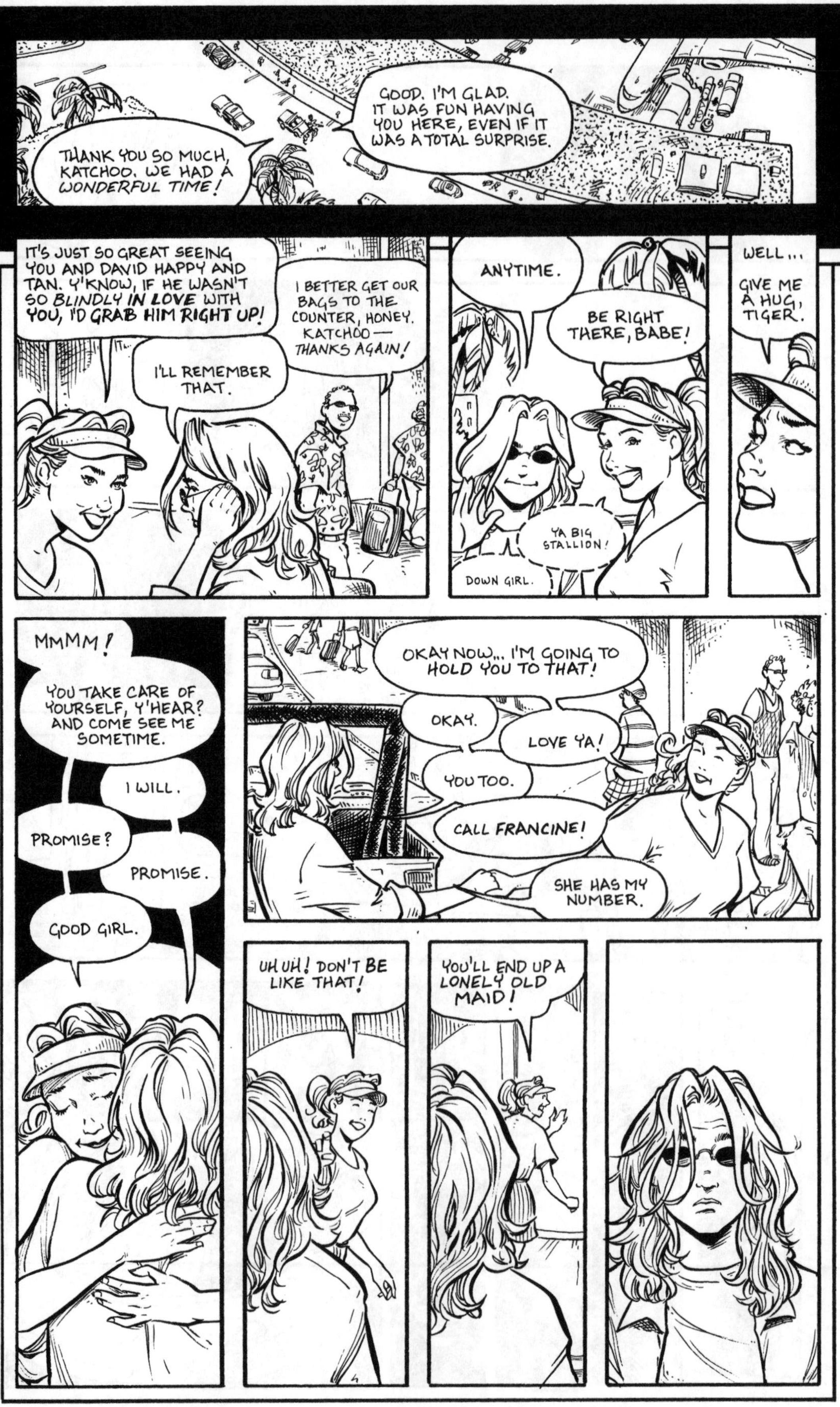
THANK YOU SO MUCH, KATCHOO. WE HAD A WONDERFUL TIME!
GOOD. I'M GLAD. IT WAS FUN HAVING YOU HERE, EVEN IF IT WAS A TOTAL SURPRISE.
IT'S JUST SO GREAT SEEING YOU AND DAVID HAPPY AND TAN. Y'KNOW, IF HE WASN'T SO BLINDLY IN LOVE WITH YOU, I'D GRAB HIM RIGHT UP!
I'LL REMEMBER THAT.
I BETTER GET OUR BAGS TO THE COUNTER, HONEY. KATCHOO— THANKS AGAIN!
ANYTIME.
BE RIGHT THERE, BABE!
YA BIG STALLION!
DOWN GIRL.
WELL...
GIVE ME A HUG, TIGER.
MMMM!
YOU TAKE CARE OF YOURSELF, Y'HEAR? AND COME SEE ME SOMETIME.
I WILL.
PROMISE?
PROMISE.
GOOD GIRL.
OKAY NOW... I'M GOING TO HOLD YOU TO THAT!
OKAY.
LOVE YA!
YOU TOO.
CALL FRANCINE!
SHE HAS MY NUMBER.
UH UH! DON'T BE LIKE THAT!
YOU'LL END UP A LONELY OLD MAID!

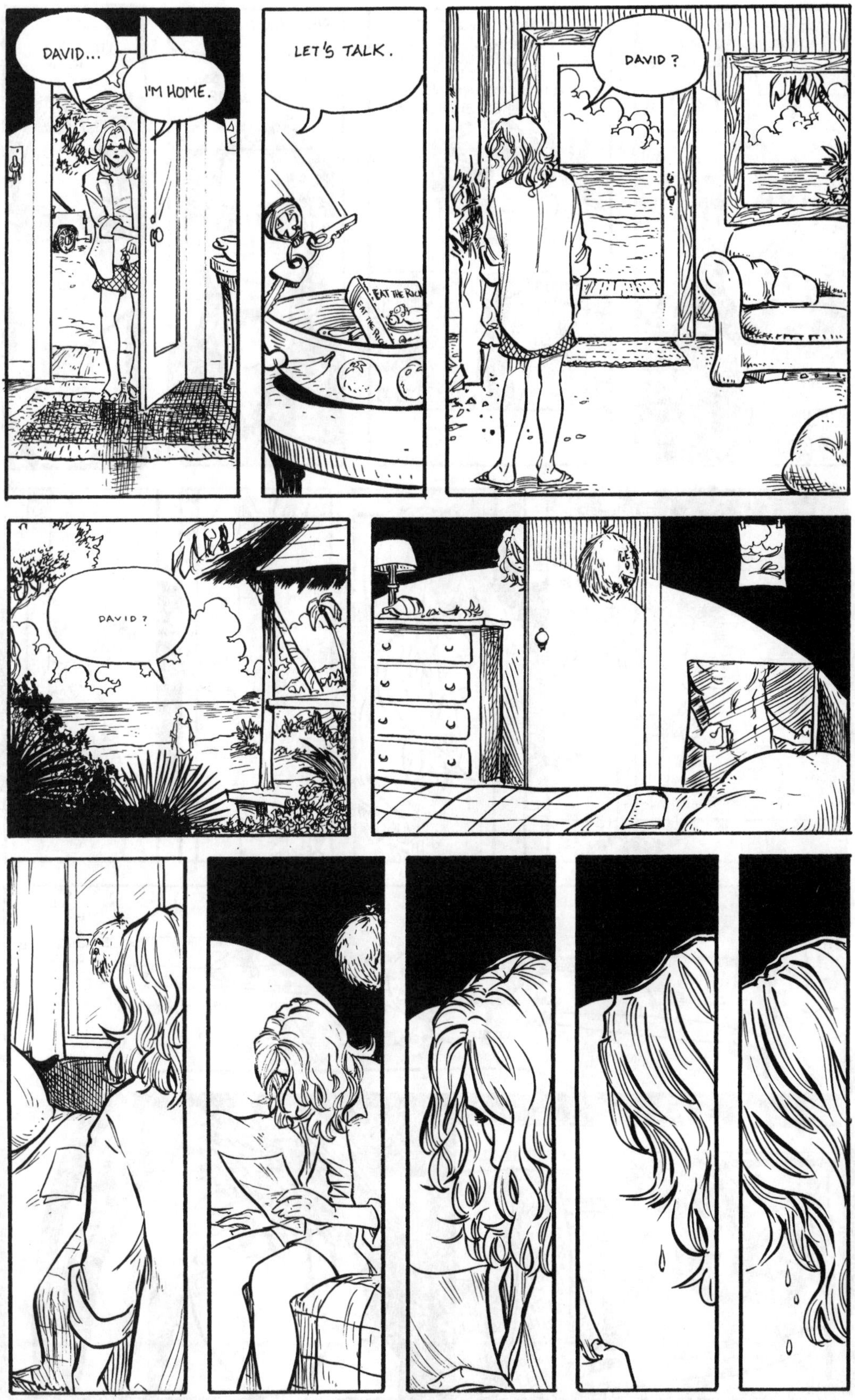
DAVID...
I'M HOME.
LET'S TALK.
EAT THE RICH
DAVID?
DAVID?

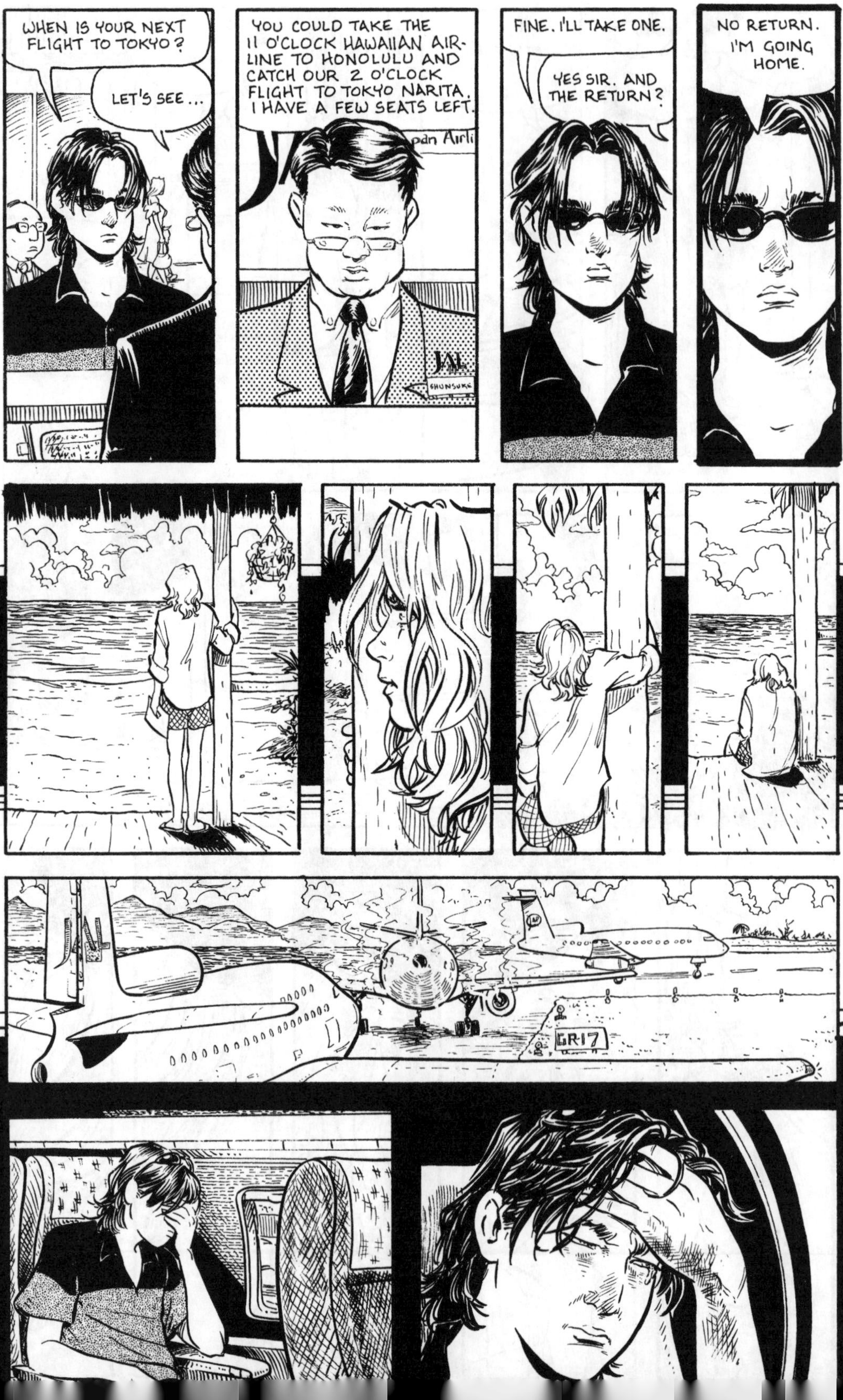

WHEN IS YOUR NEXT FLIGHT TO TOKYO?
LET'S SEE...
YOU COULD TAKE THE 11 O'CLOCK HAWAIIAN AIR-LINE TO HONOLULU AND CATCH OUR 2 O'CLOCK FLIGHT TO TOKYO NARITA. I HAVE A FEW SEATS LEFT.
SHUNSUKE
FINE. I'LL TAKE ONE.
YES SIR. AND THE RETURN?
NO RETURN. I'M GOING HOME.
GR-17

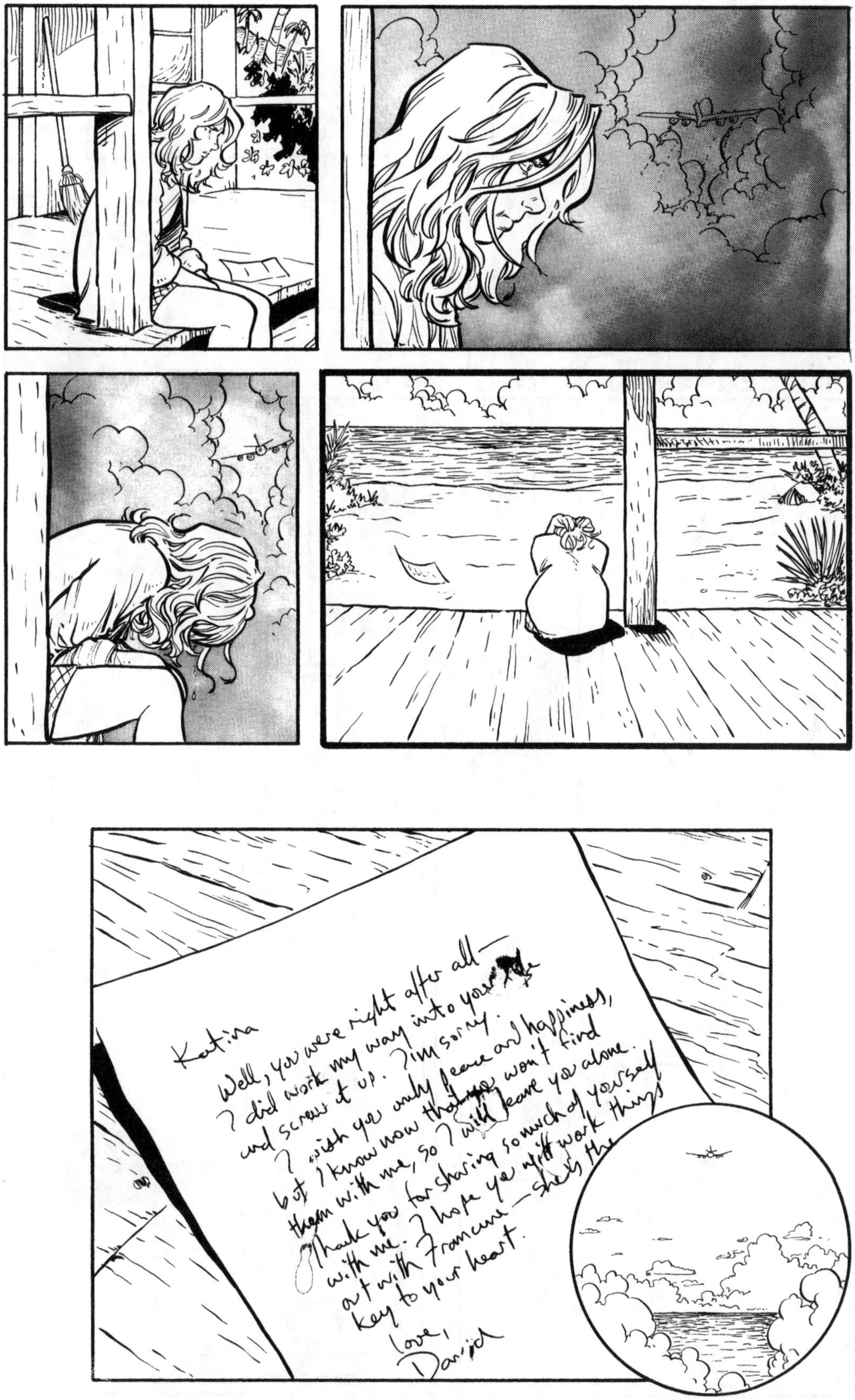
Katina
Well, you were right after all—
I did work my way into your
and screw it up. I'm sorry.
I wish you only peace and happiness,
but I know now that you won't find
them with me, so I will leave you alone.
Thank you for sharing so much of yourself
with me. I hope you will work things
out with Francine—she's the
key to your heart.
Love,
David

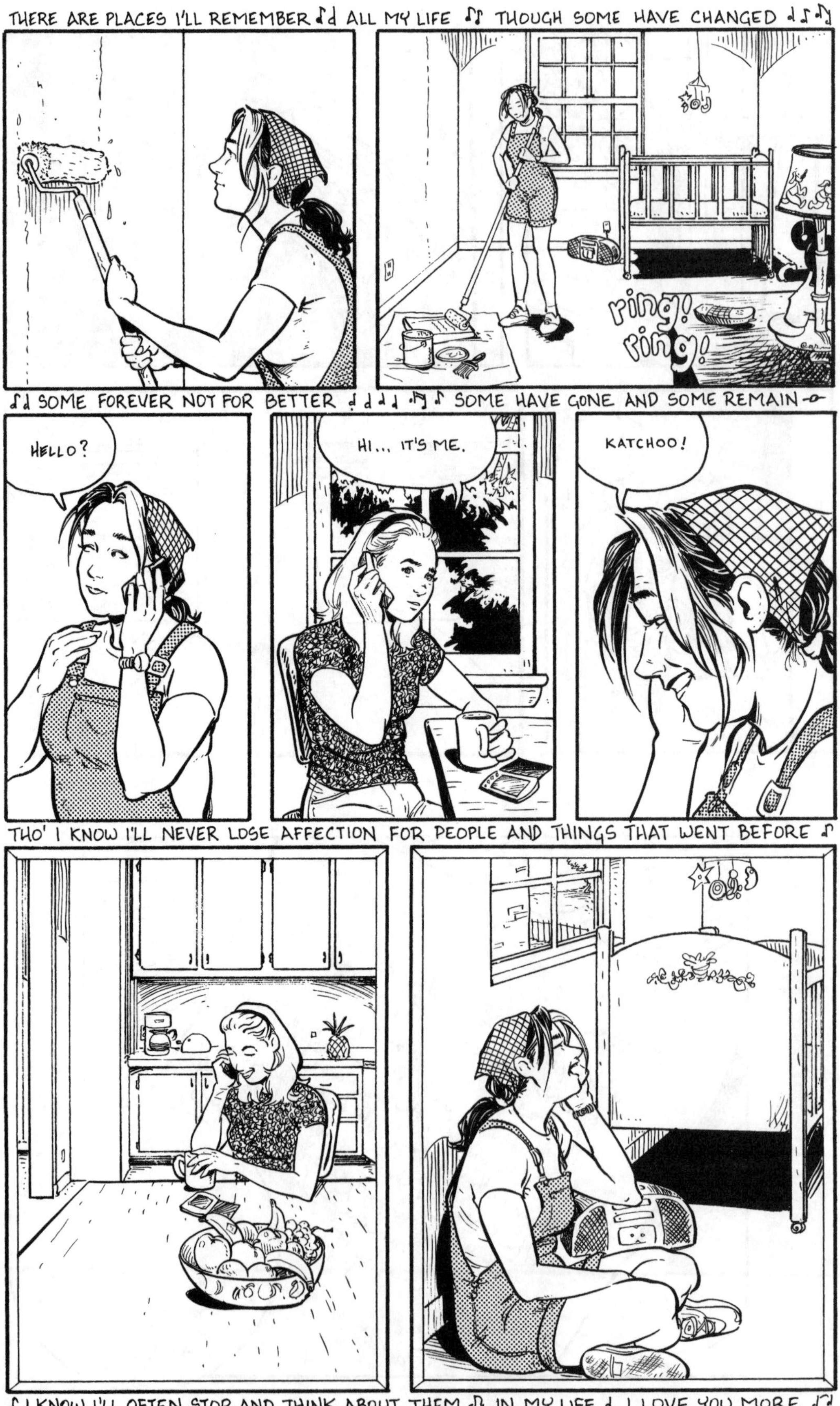

THERE ARE PLACES I'LL REMEMBER ALL MY LIFE THOUGH SOME HAVE CHANGED
ring! ring!
SOME FOREVER NOT FOR BETTER SOME HAVE GONE AND SOME REMAIN
HELLO?
HI... IT'S ME.
KATCHOO!
THO' I KNOW I'LL NEVER LOSE AFFECTION FOR PEOPLE AND THINGS THAT WENT BEFORE
I KNOW I'LL OFTEN STOP AND THINK ABOUT THEM IN MY LIFE I LOVE YOU MORE

I wake up alone at the foot of twilight
with the scent of you still in my hair,
with things left to say,
with secrets to share and
stillborn I love you's prepared.
I wake up alone in the dark,
far from the light we once had;
a tear on my cheek,
I was good for you then,
but now my reflection is bad.

Living in shadows
where the light never goes,
losing battles
to the one I'm fighting for.
Living in shadows
where the light never goes,
living shadows
dance upon my troubled soul.

I look for a candle
and then there you are.
Well I guess you were there all along.
So night turns to day
and the shadows I faced
were the promise of dreams yet to come.

Living in shadows
where the light never goes,
losing battles
to the one I'm fighting for.
Living in shadows
where the light never goes,
living shadows
dance upon my troubled soul.

Living In Shadows, by Griffin Silver, ©Ma Malai Music
from the cd Drunk Ducks

My name is Katina Choovanski. My friends, the few I have left, call me Katchoo for short. It's a contraction, see? Kat-ina Choo-vanski. My dad came up with that. He was always making words up. They say that's a sign of genius, people who make up their own words. Could have fooled me; I thought it was a lack of vocabulary. Anyway, I was so tiny when I was born my father said I was no bigger than a sneeze so he called me his little Katchoo. A little cute for a grown woman, but it's all I have left of the old man so I keep it. This is my real father I'm talking about by the way, not the asshole my mother married when I was eight years old. That would be Ace. What kind of name is that for a man: Ace? Like he's a junk yard dog or something. That's like those big boobed strippers who call themselves Montana. Ace. I guess a name like that gets you a little more respect down in cell block D... pedophiles and pushers really respect a guy named Ace. • I could go on with this for hours. In case you can't tell, I hate the guy. If I ever lay eyes on him again I will kill him on the spot. I mean it. I will kill him, any time, any place, anywhere; just kill him

and let the police take me away. There isn't enough profanity in the world to express my complete and utter contempt for that filthy son of a bitch. I'm a Scorpio with six fixed water signs— I do not forget and I do not forgive somebody who's crossed the line with me. And I would say sodomizing your 16 year old stepdaughter is crossing the line, wouldn't you? I swear to god... that is one dead man walking. Someday.... • But I didn't mean to get off on that... I'm supposed to be writing about love. Love, love. Happy face. Love. Smile. Smile. ...Smile, you cranky bitch!

Geez, reading back over what I've written, I sound like a freakin' psycho! No wonder my shrink suggested I do this. I'm sure she wants me to see what I sound like... and, yeesh! I sound like an Arnold Swarzenneger movie. Okay, so I have anger issues. My shrink— hot tomato by the way, has kind of a uniform thing going with her wardrobe: Meeoow!— she says some people have issues, I have a complete library. I paid $250 an hour for that appraisal. Apparently I have good judgement issues as well. • Anyway, the sassy lady with the uniform fetish who likes to tell people what to do with their lives told me to start keeping a journal. It's not a diary— that was pre-21st century— it's a journal. A diary will embarrass you, a journal will destroy your life... if ever found and read by anybody who even remotely knows who you are. So I guess I'd have to kill them, too. Plus you, if you're reading this. • Just kidding. • So I'm keeping this journal now and this is the very first thing I'm writing in it: I love Francine Peters. I want to marry her. I want to adopt children with her and raise them in a beautiful home in a civilized neighborhood where we could be accepted as a same sex couple. I want to wake up every morning and see her sleeping beside me, I want to take trips together, walk hand in hand through Paris and share chocolate crepes at a street stand in St. Tropez. I want to wash her hair at night and take her car in for service, I want to shop for furniture together and let her buy anything she wants. I want to kiss her on her birthday for the rest of her life, I want to wipe her tears and make her laugh, I want to rub her feet at night and tell her the entire universe revolves around her. I love that woman. Everytime I see her I just want to grab her and never let go. Heaven is me and her, on a tropical island, with silk sheets. • Unfortunately, she doesn't feel the same way towards me. She's told me so, several times. So.... anger issues. What do you do when the love of your life is another woman... and she just can't find it within herself to go there with you? Anger issues. Our relationship has been a roller-coaster ride. A lot of history... too much for one journal. But today I'm flying back to see her after months apart. We've been talking on the phone; she told me she's pregnant but she's not going to marry the father. She asked me to come visit her in Houston, so of course I grabbed the first available plane and... here I am. We're landing. I don't know what to expect. All I know is I love her. God help me, I love that woman with all my heart. Now if I can only keep that to myself maybe she won't run away from me this time. Wheels touched ground. What do I have to lose? Everything. • Taxi to the gate. I'd forgotten how flat Houston is. Where are my beautiful Hawaiian hills? Heart suddenly fluttered like I'd just been injected with pure caffeine. Crap, this is what I was afraid of... that I'd be nervous and act weird. That's all I need is to walk up the ramp and act like a speed freak— Hey, Katchoo, we barely recognized you; you look like crap! What's with the twitching and heavy sweating? You're acting like a fat man in a little boat. • Okay, so here's how I'm going to get through this: I'm going to calmly walk off this plane and see Francine for the first time in months. We'll say hi, how are ya', let's go get a bite to eat... she'll show me her baby room and I'll say it's so cuuuute and then I'll go to my hotel room, lay on the bed in my sweats, find a ball game on the tube and order a six pack of Budweisers from room service with those little crunchy crab finger appetizers. I'll get drunk, burp myself to sleep, and when I wake up I'll go home. No complaints. I came, I was nice, she broke my heart telling me about the men in her life, I'll smile and say, It'll work out, Francie. And... like that. It's all in your point of view, Katchoo... 6 billion people in the world will go to sleep tonight without the slightest worry about what Francine Peters will do with the rest of her life and who she'll do it with. Why can't you? It's all in your point of view. Point of view. Just walk in, look her straight in the eye and say hi like she was any old skank off the street. Pay no mind to those big brown eyes or pale slender fingers or deep red lips or... Right. • Note to self: call shrink when you get back and ask her out. Tell her to wear the sailor outfit.

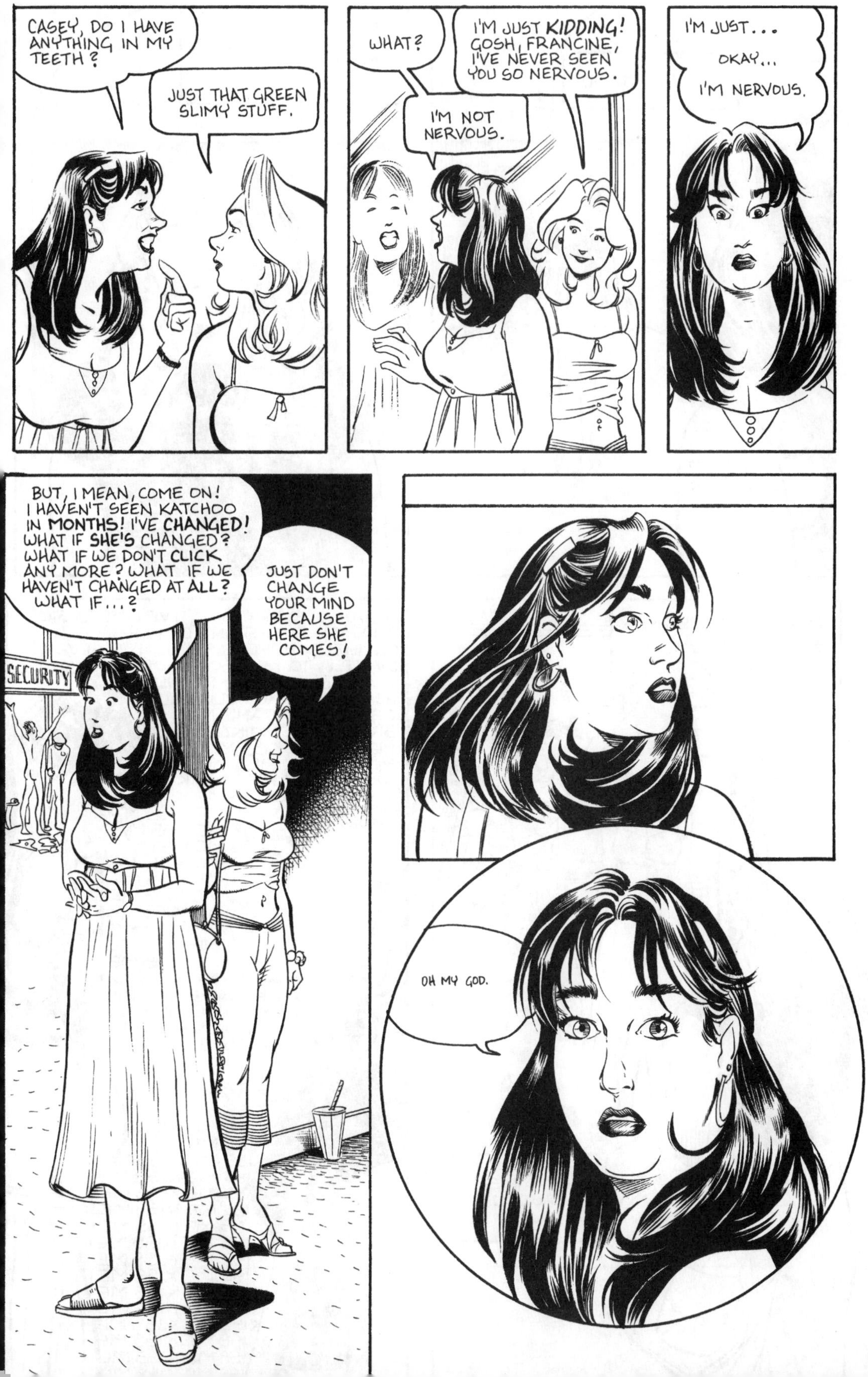

CASEY, DO I HAVE ANYTHING IN MY TEETH?
JUST THAT GREEN SLIMY STUFF.
WHAT?
I'M JUST KIDDING! GOSH, FRANCINE, I'VE NEVER SEEN YOU SO NERVOUS.
I'M NOT NERVOUS.
I'M JUST... OKAY... I'M NERVOUS.
BUT, I MEAN, COME ON! I HAVEN'T SEEN KATCHOO IN MONTHS! I'VE CHANGED! WHAT IF SHE'S CHANGED? WHAT IF WE DON'T CLICK ANY MORE? WHAT IF WE HAVEN'T CHANGED AT ALL? WHAT IF...?
JUST DON'T CHANGE YOUR MIND BECAUSE HERE SHE COMES!
SECURITY
OH MY GOD.

DAMN

SHE'S **BEAUTIFUL**!

MORE BEAUTIFUL THAN I REMEMBERED. MORE BEAUTIFUL THAN MY DREAMS.

AND THERE SHE STANDS WAITING FOR ME, LIKE A LIGHT AT THE END OF THE TUNNEL.

MY ANGEL.

MY DAMN SHE'S BEAUTIFUL ANGEL.

IT TAKES EVERYTHING I'VE GOT TO STOP AND STAND IN FRONT OF HER LIKE A CIVILIZED HUMAN BEING. I'VE NEVER WANTED TO KISS SOMEBODY SO BAD IN ALL MY LIFE. ALL I COULD HEAR WAS THE POUNDING OF MY HEART AND MY BRAIN SCREAMING KISS ME KISS ME KISS ME KISS ME K

KISS ME KISS ME K
KISS ME KISS ME K
KISS ME KISS ME K
ISS ME KISS M
ISS ME KISS I
ME KISS ME
ME KISS ME K
ME KISS ME K
ME KISS ME KISS
SME KISS ME KIS
SME KISS ME KI
S ME KISS ME K
1E KISS ME KISS ME K
1E KISS ME KISS ME K
1E KISS ME KISS ME K
1E KISS ME KISS ME K
E KISS ME KISS ME
E KISS ME KISS ME
E KISS ME KISS M
KISS ME KISS M
KISS ME KISS M
KISS ME KISS M
KISS ME KISS N
ISS ME KISS ME
ISS ME KISS ME K
KISS ME KISS ME K
KISS ME KISS ME K
KISS ME KISS ME K
KISS ME KISS ME
KISS ME KISS ME
KISS ME KISS ME
ISS ME KISS ME
ISS ME KISS ME

HI.
HI.
SO...
YEAH.
MMM ?
MM HMM.
CAN I...
CAN I BUY YOU DINNER?
I MADE LASAGNA.
DID YOU MAKE WINE?
NO.
THEN I'LL BUY THAT.
HELLO?! YOO HOO!
HOORAY! YOU'RE BACK!
HI! OH, I'M GLAD TO SEE YOU, TOO!
YOU CAN BUY ME DINNER!
AM I INVISIBLE? CAN ANYBODY HEAR ME?
I CAN HEAR THAT OUTFIT!
DON'T TALK TO THE DADAISTS, DEAR.
USE YOUR WORDS GIRLS — TALK ENGLISH!
OR LASAGNA'S FINE. WHATEVER.
HEY! DID YOU GUYS ENTER THE TWILIGHT ZONE? HELLOO?
I SAW HOW TO MAKE WINE ON THE FOOD CHANNEL ONCE!

OKAY, I DON'T KNOW WHAT YOU TWO ARE DOING BUT I'M PRETTY SURE IT'S ILLEGAL IN THE BIBLE BELT! C'MON, ROMEO AND JULIET, LET'S **VAMOOSE!**

WE'RE JUST MAKING DINNER PLANS.

UH HUH... I WISH I HAD PLANS LIKE THAT!

≈ SNORT! ≈

WHOA! CHECK OUT THE BABE IN THE HOT PANTS!

OH, HER? SHE'S AN EX-PLAYBOY PLAYMATE.

GET OUT OF TOWN! FOR REAL?

SURE! WE USED TO GO OUT. SHE WAS CRAZY ABOUT ME, BUT I HAD TO CUT HER LOOSE— TOO CLINGY!

SO THAT'S THE **THIRD** PLAYMATE YOU'VE BAGGED! MAN, HOW DO YOU KEEP SCORIN' THE **SPECIAL TAIL?**

THE CLASSY DAME'S LOVE A BEAUTIFUL MIND, WILLY— THAT AND A **V8 CAMARO!**

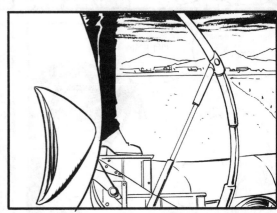

WELCOME TO JAPAN, TAMBI-SAN.

I HOPE YOU WILL FIND TIME FOR **PLEASURE** AS WELL AS BUSINESS DURING YOUR STAY WITH US.

BELIEVE ME, MY BUSINESS HERE **WILL BE A PLEASURE!**

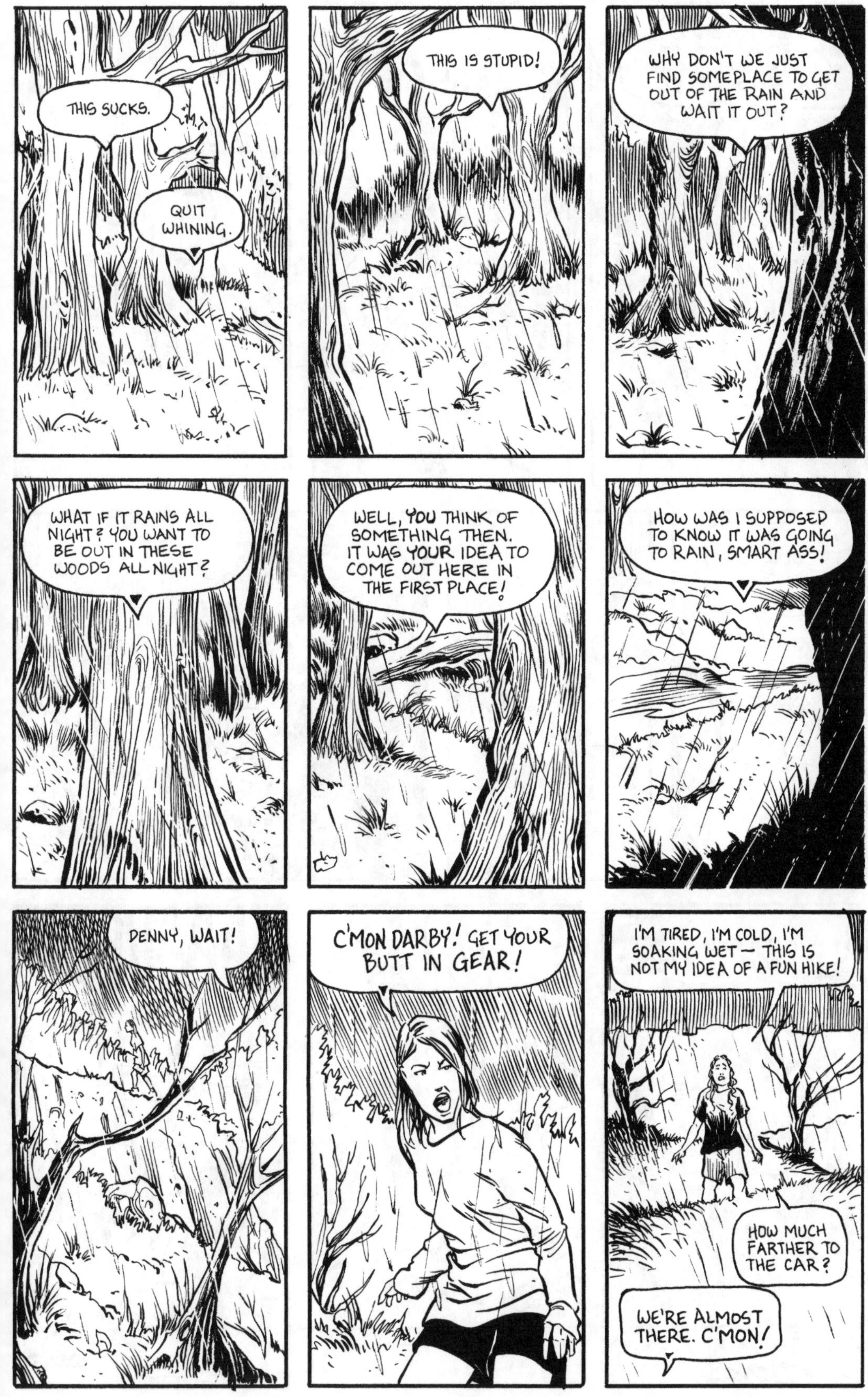
THIS SUCKS.
QUIT WHINING.
THIS IS STUPID!
WHY DON'T WE JUST FIND SOMEPLACE TO GET OUT OF THE RAIN AND WAIT IT OUT?
WHAT IF IT RAINS ALL NIGHT? YOU WANT TO BE OUT IN THESE WOODS ALL NIGHT?
WELL, YOU THINK OF SOMETHING THEN. IT WAS YOUR IDEA TO COME OUT HERE IN THE FIRST PLACE!
HOW WAS I SUPPOSED TO KNOW IT WAS GOING TO RAIN, SMART ASS!
DENNY, WAIT!
C'MON DARBY! GET YOUR BUTT IN GEAR!
I'M TIRED, I'M COLD, I'M SOAKING WET — THIS IS NOT MY IDEA OF A FUN HIKE!
HOW MUCH FARTHER TO THE CAR?
WE'RE ALMOST THERE. C'MON!

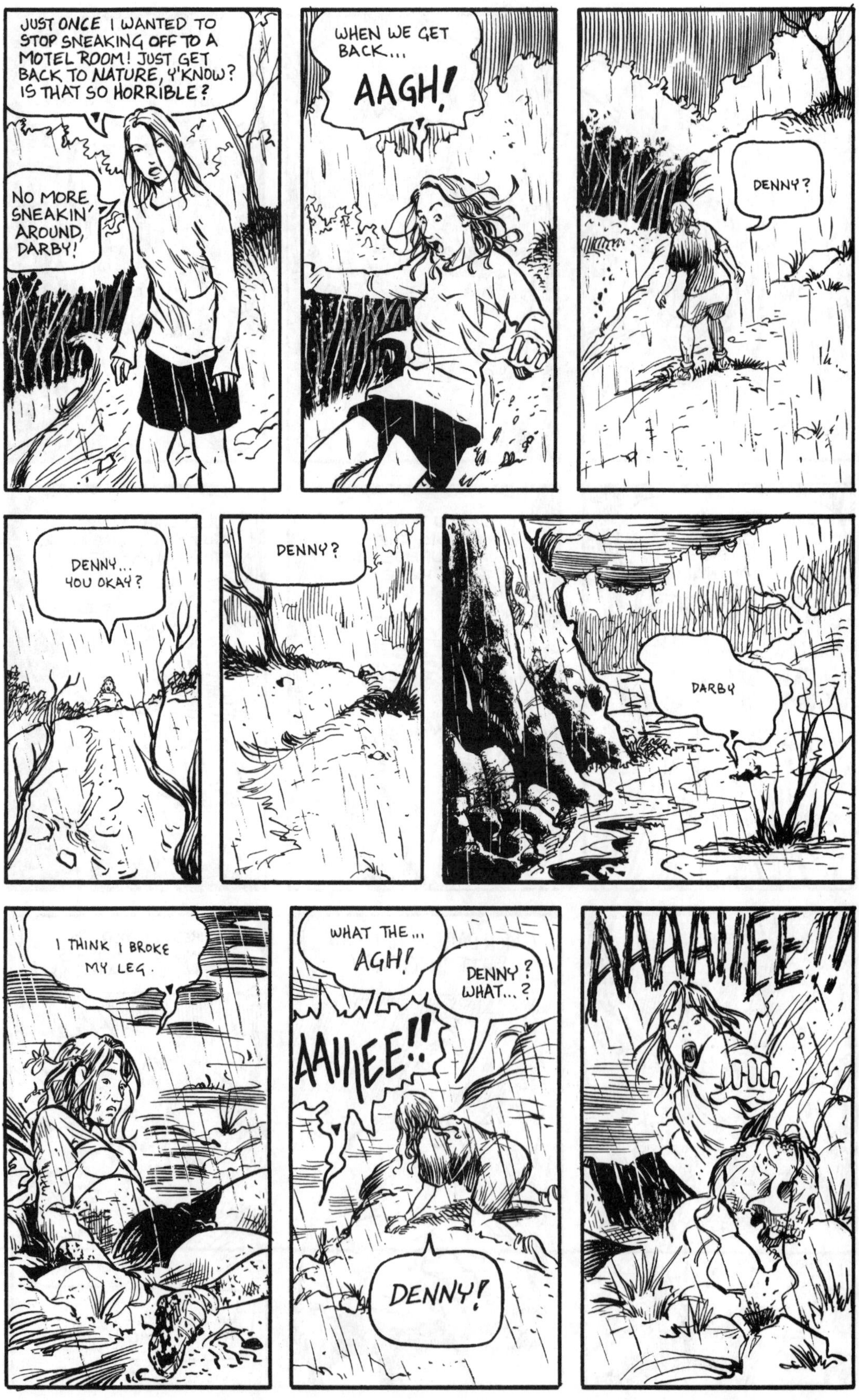
JUST ONCE I WANTED TO STOP SNEAKING OFF TO A MOTEL ROOM! JUST GET BACK TO NATURE, Y'KNOW? IS THAT SO HORRIBLE?
NO MORE SNEAKIN' AROUND, DARBY!
WHEN WE GET BACK...
AAGH!
DENNY?
DENNY... YOU OKAY?
DENNY?
DARBY
I THINK I BROKE MY LEG.
WHAT THE... AGH!
DENNY? WHAT...?
AAIIEE!!
DENNY!
AAAAIIEE!!

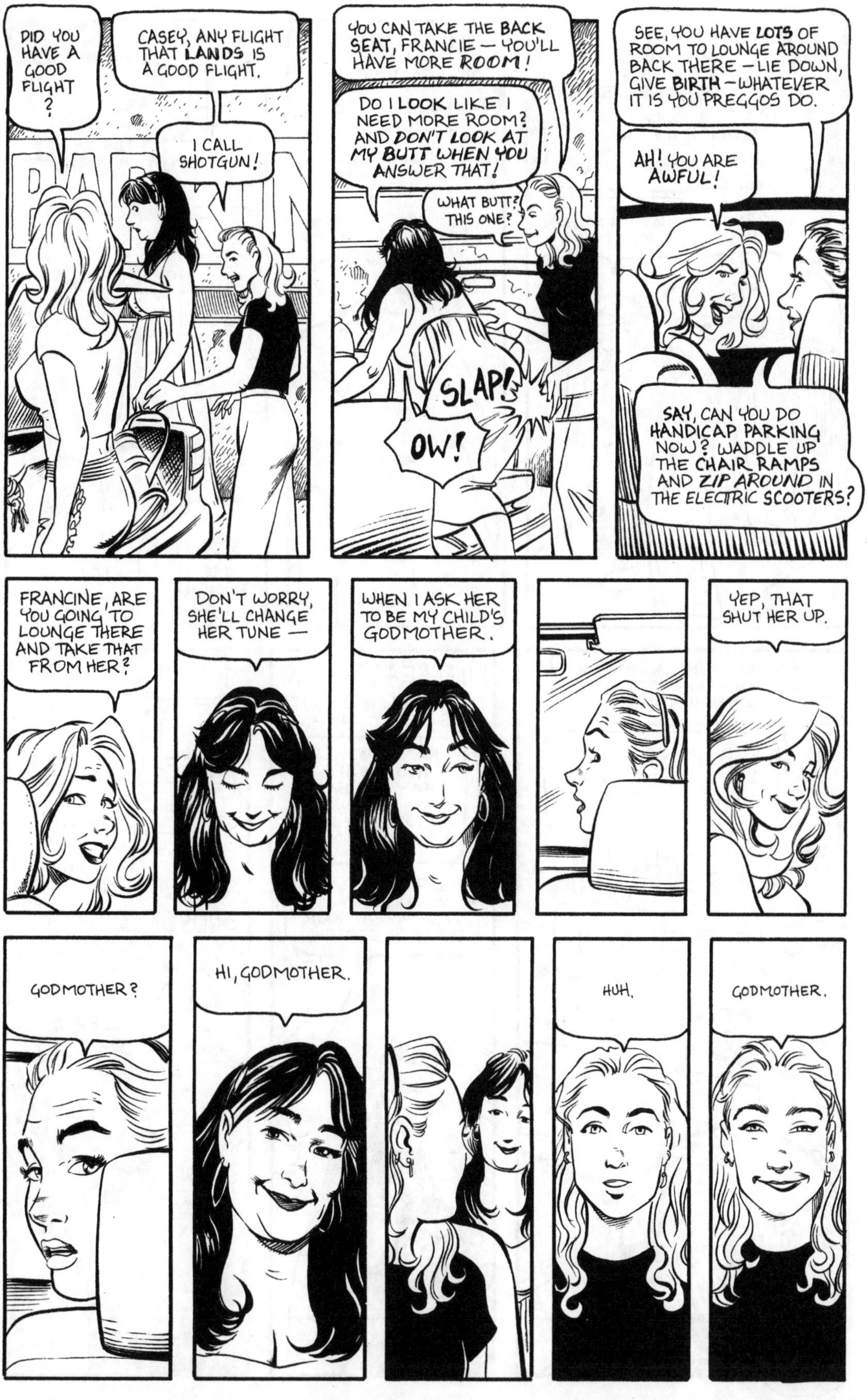
DID YOU HAVE A GOOD FLIGHT?
CASEY, ANY FLIGHT THAT LANDS IS A GOOD FLIGHT.
I CALL SHOTGUN!
YOU CAN TAKE THE BACK SEAT, FRANCIE — YOU'LL HAVE MORE ROOM!
DO I LOOK LIKE I NEED MORE ROOM? AND DON'T LOOK AT MY BUTT WHEN YOU ANSWER THAT!
WHAT BUTT? THIS ONE?
SLAP!
OW!
SEE, YOU HAVE LOTS OF ROOM TO LOUNGE AROUND BACK THERE — LIE DOWN, GIVE BIRTH — WHATEVER IT IS YOU PREGGOS DO.
AH! YOU ARE AWFUL!
SAY, CAN YOU DO HANDICAP PARKING NOW? WADDLE UP THE CHAIR RAMPS AND ZIP AROUND IN THE ELECTRIC SCOOTERS?
FRANCINE, ARE YOU GOING TO LOUNGE THERE AND TAKE THAT FROM HER?
DON'T WORRY, SHE'LL CHANGE HER TUNE —
WHEN I ASK HER TO BE MY CHILD'S GODMOTHER.
YEP, THAT SHUT HER UP.
GODMOTHER?
HI, GODMOTHER.
HUH.
GODMOTHER.

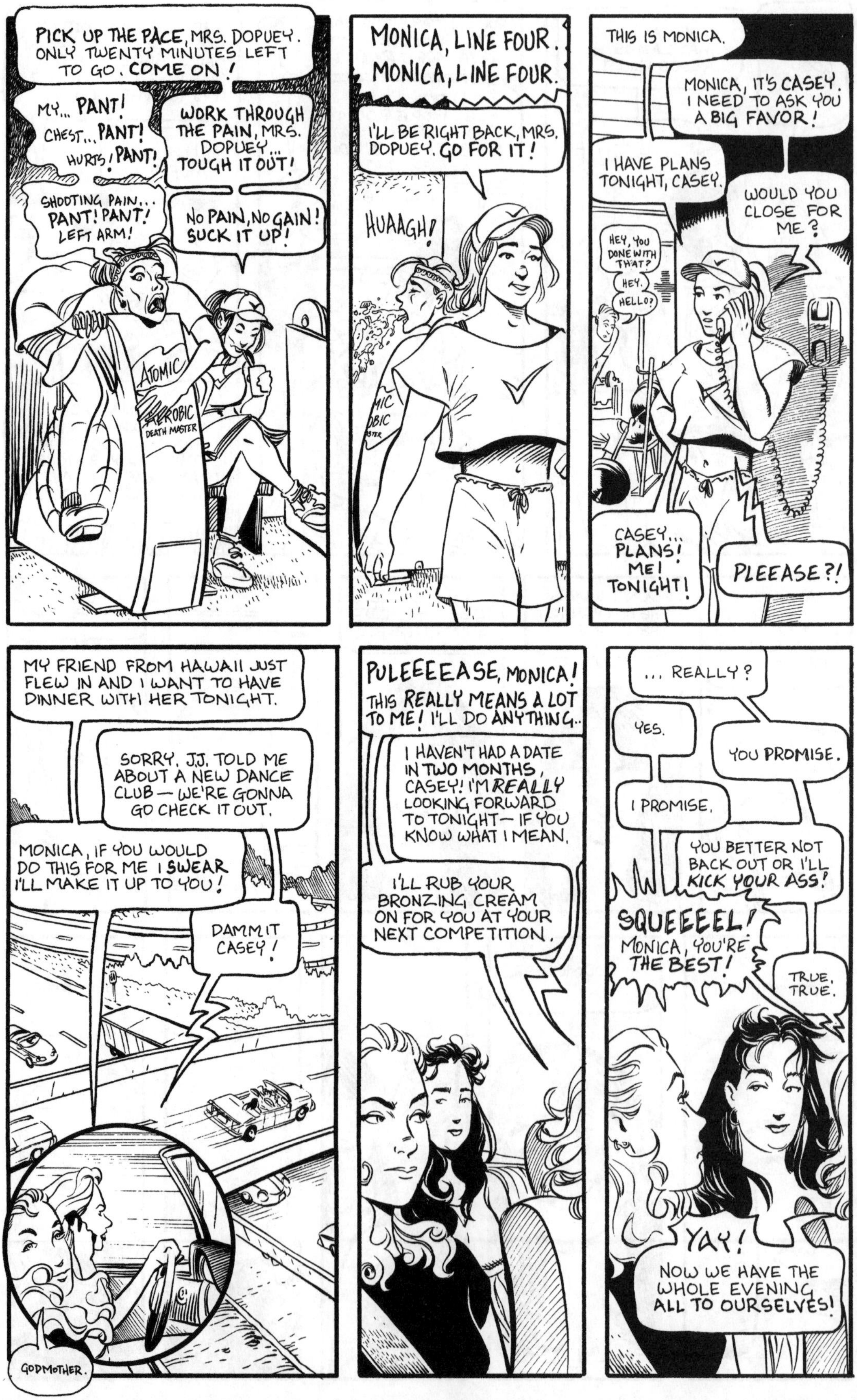
PICK UP THE PACE, MRS. DOPUEY. ONLY TWENTY MINUTES LEFT TO GO. COME ON!
MY... PANT! CHEST... PANT! HURTS! PANT!
WORK THROUGH THE PAIN, MRS. DOPUEY... TOUGH IT OUT!
SHOOTING PAIN... PANT! PANT! LEFT ARM!
NO PAIN, NO GAIN! SUCK IT UP!
ATOMIC AEROBIC DEATH MASTER
MONICA, LINE FOUR. MONICA, LINE FOUR.
I'LL BE RIGHT BACK, MRS. DOPUEY. GO FOR IT!
HUAAGH!
THIS IS MONICA.
MONICA, IT'S CASEY. I NEED TO ASK YOU A BIG FAVOR!
I HAVE PLANS TONIGHT, CASEY.
WOULD YOU CLOSE FOR ME?
HEY, YOU DONE WITH THAT?
HEY.
HELLO?
CASEY... PLANS! ME! TONIGHT!
PLEEASE?!
MY FRIEND FROM HAWAII JUST FLEW IN AND I WANT TO HAVE DINNER WITH HER TONIGHT.
SORRY. J.J. TOLD ME ABOUT A NEW DANCE CLUB — WE'RE GONNA GO CHECK IT OUT.
MONICA, IF YOU WOULD DO THIS FOR ME I SWEAR I'LL MAKE IT UP TO YOU!
DAMMIT CASEY!
GODMOTHER.
PULEEEEASE, MONICA! THIS REALLY MEANS A LOT TO ME! I'LL DO ANYTHING..
I HAVEN'T HAD A DATE IN TWO MONTHS, CASEY! I'M REALLY LOOKING FORWARD TO TONIGHT— IF YOU KNOW WHAT I MEAN.
I'LL RUB YOUR BRONZING CREAM ON FOR YOU AT YOUR NEXT COMPETITION.
... REALLY?
YES.
YOU PROMISE.
I PROMISE.
YOU BETTER NOT BACK OUT OR I'LL KICK YOUR ASS!
SQUEEEEL! MONICA, YOU'RE THE BEST!
TRUE. TRUE.
YAY! NOW WE HAVE THE WHOLE EVENING ALL TO OURSELVES!

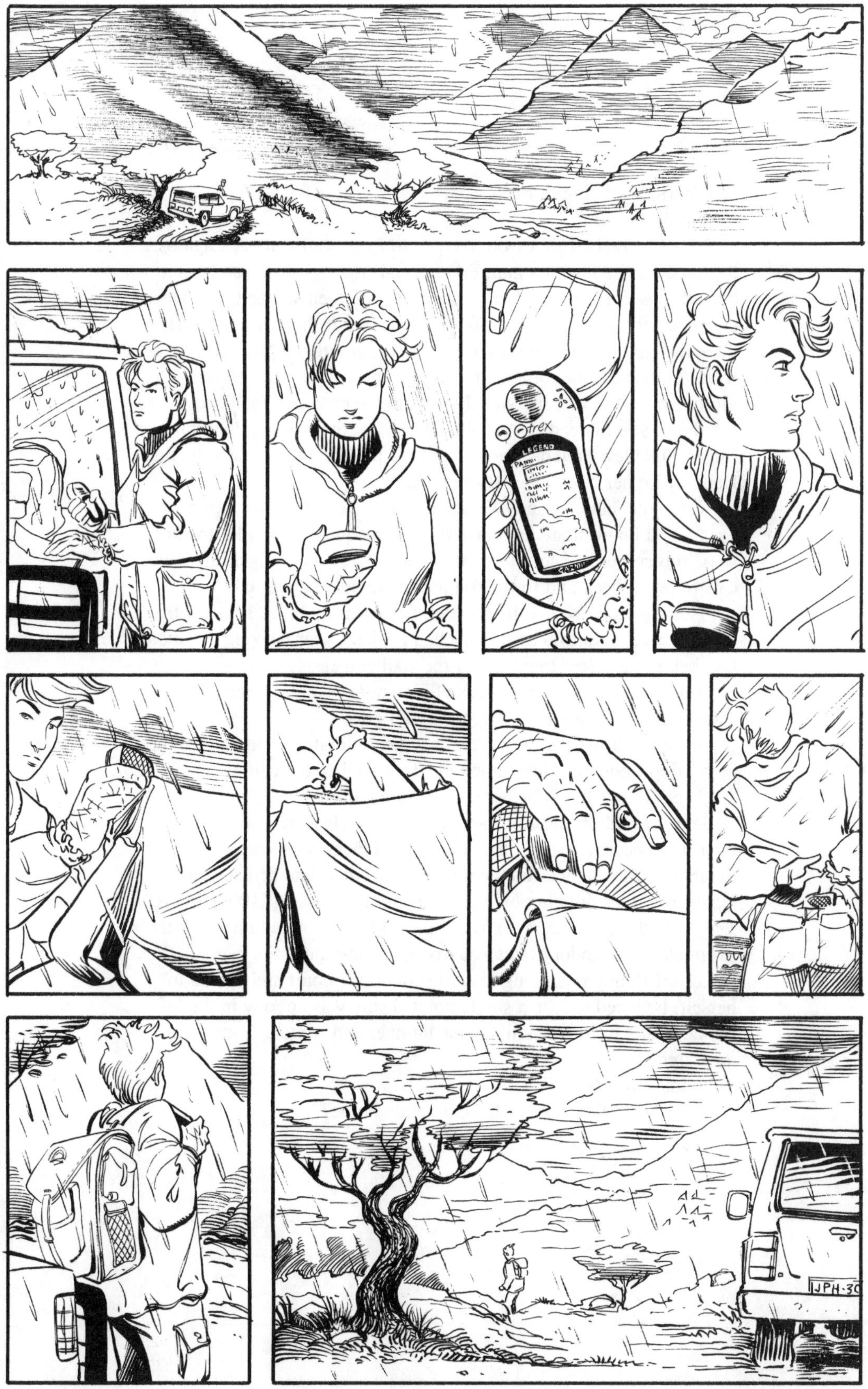
trex
LEGEND
JPH-30

"Fourteen serving thirteen."

"Don't rub it in."

WHAP! The ball shot from racquet to front wall and back again like a bullet fired from a gun. FBI Special Agent Sara Bryan forced herself to wait for the ball to come to her and then stepped into her swing, catching the blue blur as it ricocheted off the sidewall barely three inches from the ground. Her return shot hugged the side wall as it flew into the front corner, struck the front wall an inch off the ground and died, limping weakly back to the center of the floor.

"Bang, you're dead" Sara said, pointing at the ball with her index finger. She blew pretend smoke from her pretend barrel and smiled at Danny with her best James Bond look.

"Cute, real cute," Danny Victorino said, sweat dripping into his eyes. "You know, there are other shots in racquetball besides the kill shot. You could try one sometime. Then we could do this thing they call volley— back and forth. You may have heard about it."

"Not my style. You really shouldn't be wearing black socks with those shoes," Sara said as she reached for her pager buzzing for attention behind the clear Plexiglas of the wall cubicle.

Danny pulled up the pant legs of his gray sweats and bent over to inspect his feet. "What? Black goes with gray."

"I need to take this." Sarah grabbed her cell phone and opened the heavy door mounted flush along the back wall of the court.

"Yeah, fine. I'll just be here… practicing my volley."

Sara stepped off the court and let the door close behind her. Two men stood nearby wiping their flushed red faces with white towels. Sarah unconsciously sized them up to be in their late fifties, and in leadership roles, judging by their manicured nails and $100 haircuts. She walked across the room to a spiral stairway leading up to a loft overlooking the indoor tennis courts. Climbing the stairs two at a time she heard Danny practicing his kill shot on the court and smiled to herself; he hated to lose a single point. There was nobody in the loft so she dialed Keith Rankin's home number and waited. A little girl answered.

"Rankin residence."

"Hi. This is Sara Bryan. Is your daddy home?"

The sound of the phone dropping on the table rattled in Sara's ear. In the background Sara heard the little girl running, "Daddy... telephone!" Muffled voices followed, then the girl running back to the phone pursued by heavy footsteps on wood floors.

"Just a minute, please," the girl giggled into the phone before dropping it again. Sara smiled. She heard the sound of the receiver being lifted from the tabletop, then a man's voice, deep and flat with a midwestern accent, "Hello?"

"Mr. Rankin, It's Sara Bryan."

"I just got a call from our office in New York, Bryan. Two hikers found a human skull in a remote area of upstate New York. I want you to go up there tomorrow morning and look into it."

"Yes sir. Any particular reason why?"

"They were less than a mile from Sal Tucciani's summer house."

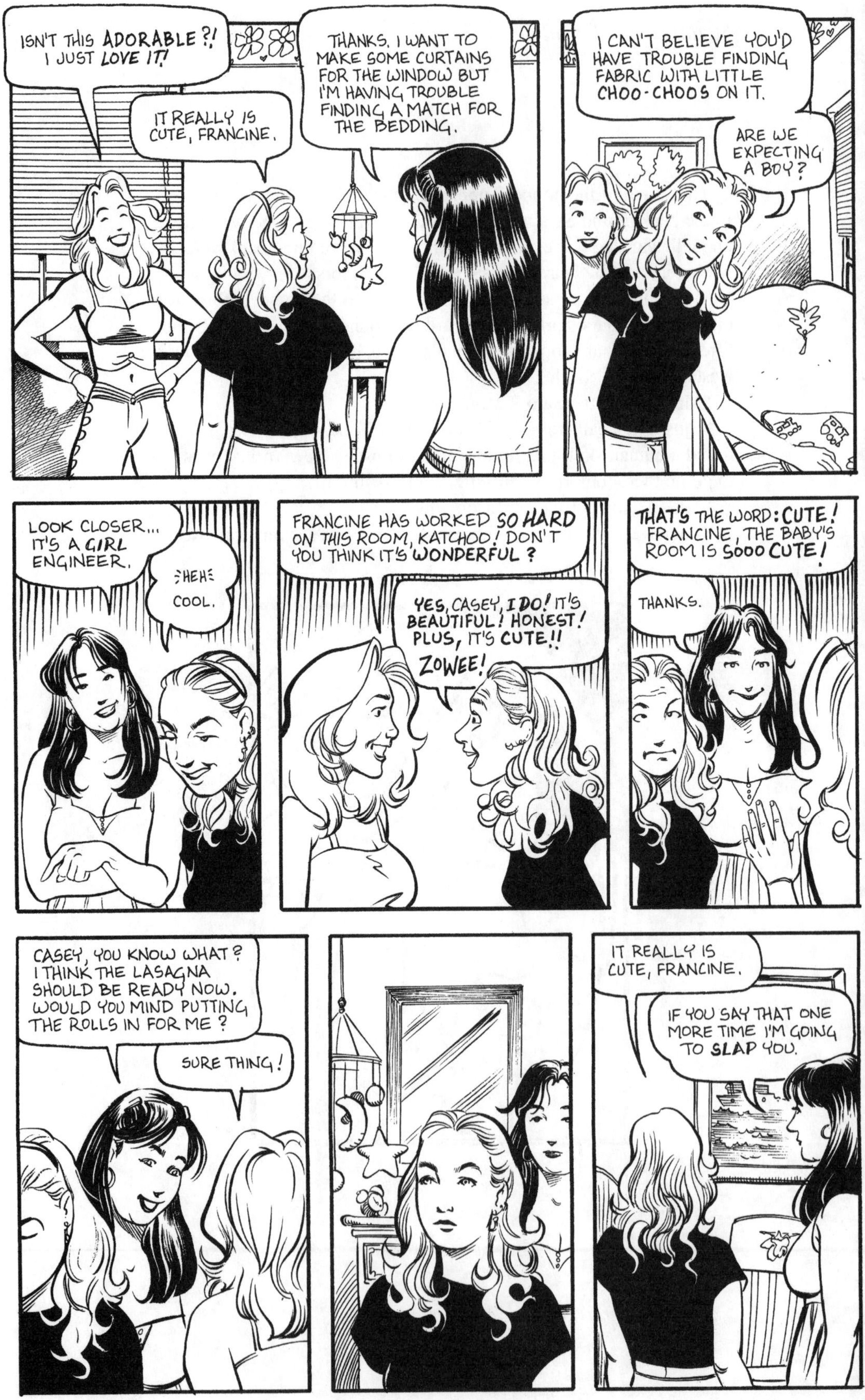
ISN'T THIS ADORABLE ?! I JUST LOVE IT!
IT REALLY IS CUTE, FRANCINE.
THANKS. I WANT TO MAKE SOME CURTAINS FOR THE WINDOW BUT I'M HAVING TROUBLE FINDING A MATCH FOR THE BEDDING.
I CAN'T BELIEVE YOU'D HAVE TROUBLE FINDING FABRIC WITH LITTLE CHOO-CHOOS ON IT.
ARE WE EXPECTING A BOY?
LOOK CLOSER... IT'S A GIRL ENGINEER.
HEH COOL.
FRANCINE HAS WORKED SO HARD ON THIS ROOM, KATCHOO! DON'T YOU THINK IT'S WONDERFUL ?
YES, CASEY, I DO! IT'S BEAUTIFUL! HONEST! PLUS, IT'S CUTE!!
ZOWEE!
THAT'S THE WORD: CUTE! FRANCINE, THE BABY'S ROOM IS SOOO CUTE!
THANKS.
CASEY, YOU KNOW WHAT? I THINK THE LASAGNA SHOULD BE READY NOW. WOULD YOU MIND PUTTING THE ROLLS IN FOR ME?
SURE THING!
IT REALLY IS CUTE, FRANCINE.
IF YOU SAY THAT ONE MORE TIME I'M GOING TO SLAP YOU.

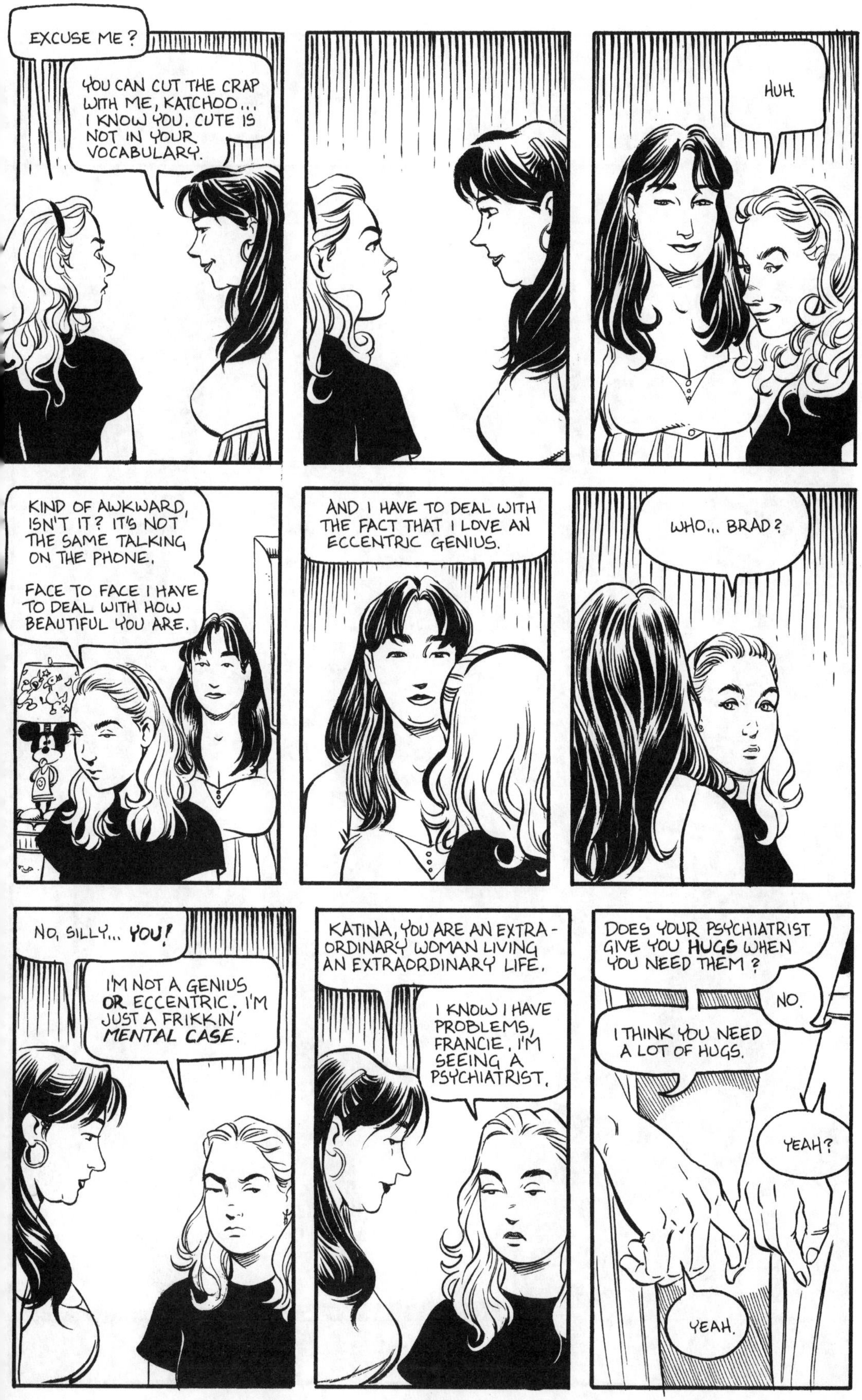

EXCUSE ME?
YOU CAN CUT THE CRAP WITH ME, KATCHOO... I KNOW YOU. CUTE IS NOT IN YOUR VOCABULARY.
HUH.
KIND OF AWKWARD, ISN'T IT? IT'S NOT THE SAME TALKING ON THE PHONE.
FACE TO FACE I HAVE TO DEAL WITH HOW BEAUTIFUL YOU ARE.
AND I HAVE TO DEAL WITH THE FACT THAT I LOVE AN ECCENTRIC GENIUS.
WHO... BRAD?
NO, SILLY... YOU!
I'M NOT A GENIUS OR ECCENTRIC. I'M JUST A FRIKKIN' MENTAL CASE.
KATINA, YOU ARE AN EXTRA-ORDINARY WOMAN LIVING AN EXTRAORDINARY LIFE.
I KNOW I HAVE PROBLEMS, FRANCIE. I'M SEEING A PSYCHIATRIST.
DOES YOUR PSYCHIATRIST GIVE YOU HUGS WHEN YOU NEED THEM?
NO.
I THINK YOU NEED A LOT OF HUGS.
YEAH?
YEAH.

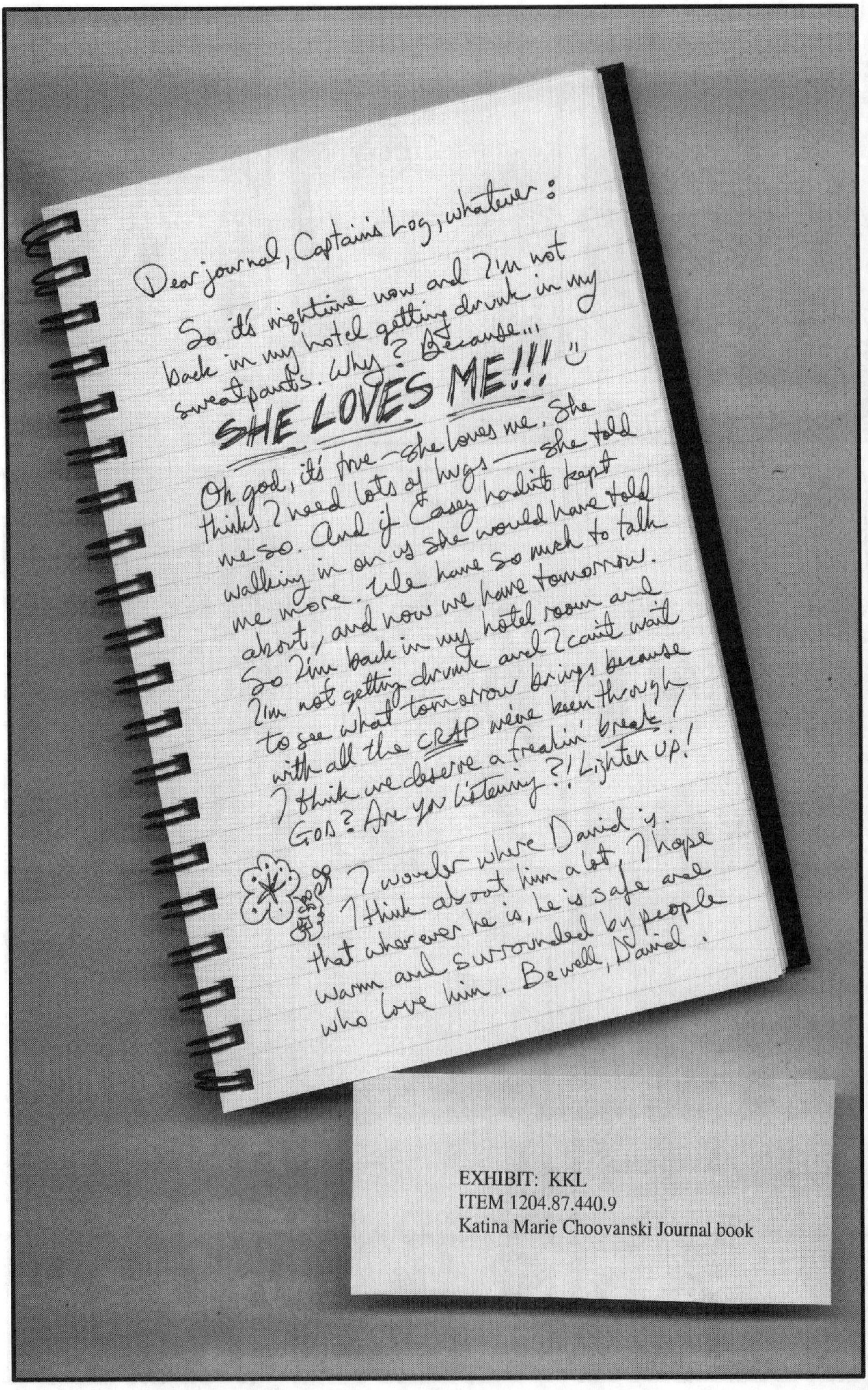
Dear journal, Captain's Log, whatever:
So it's nighttime now and I'm not
back in my hotel getting drunk in my
sweatpants. Why? Because...
SHE LOVES ME!!! :)
Oh god, it's true—she loves me. She
thinks I need lots of hugs—she told
me so. And if Casey hadn't kept
walking in on us she would have told
me more. We have so much to talk
about, and now we have tomorrow.
So I'm back in my hotel room and
I'm not getting drunk and I can't wait
to see what tomorrow brings because
with all the CRAP we've been through
I think we deserve a freakin' break!
GOD? Are you listening?! Lighten up!
I wonder where David is.
I think about him a lot. I hope
that wherever he is, he is safe and
warm and surrounded by people
who love him. Be well, David.
EXHIBIT: KKL
ITEM 1204.87.440.9
Katina Marie Choovanski Journal book

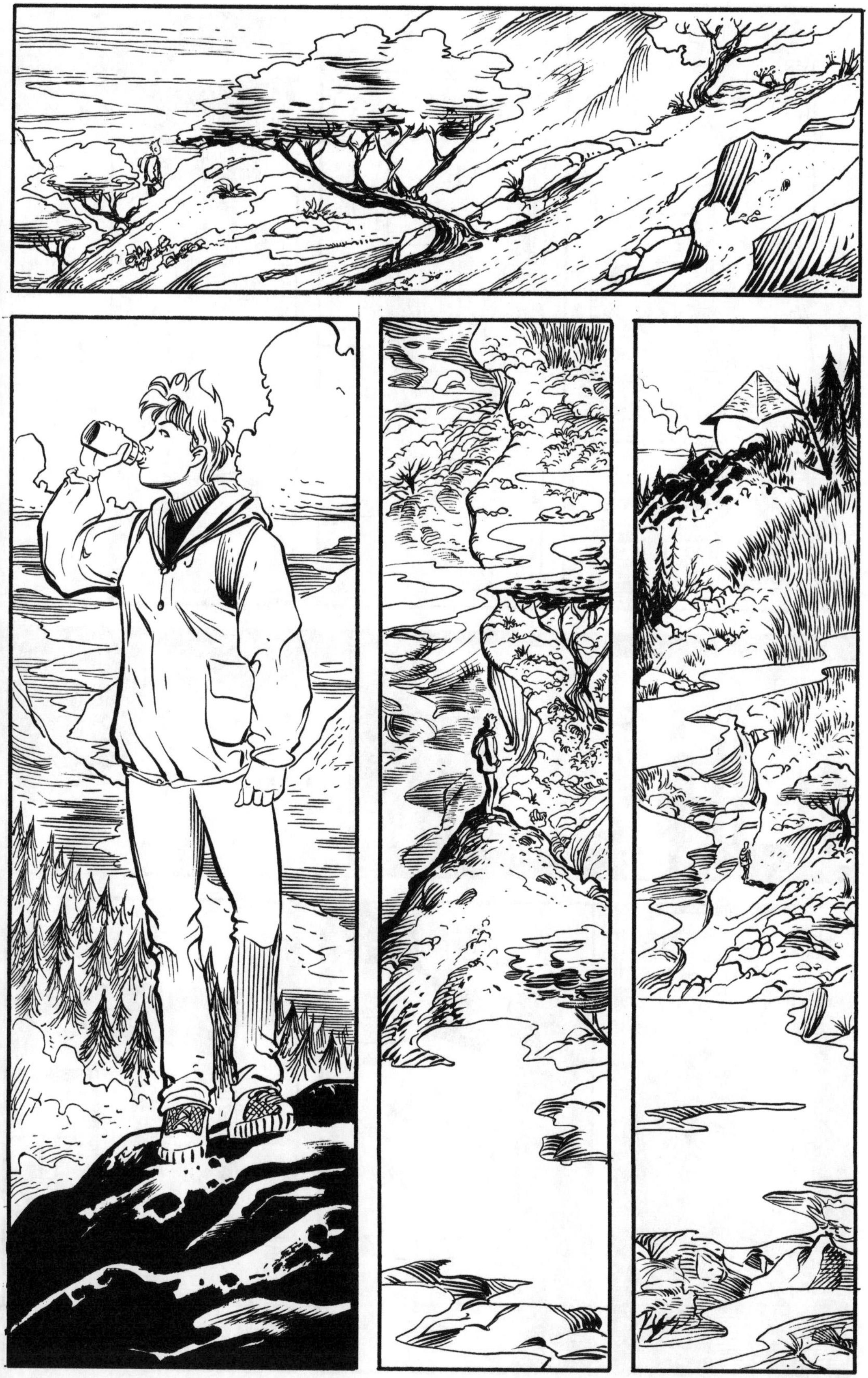

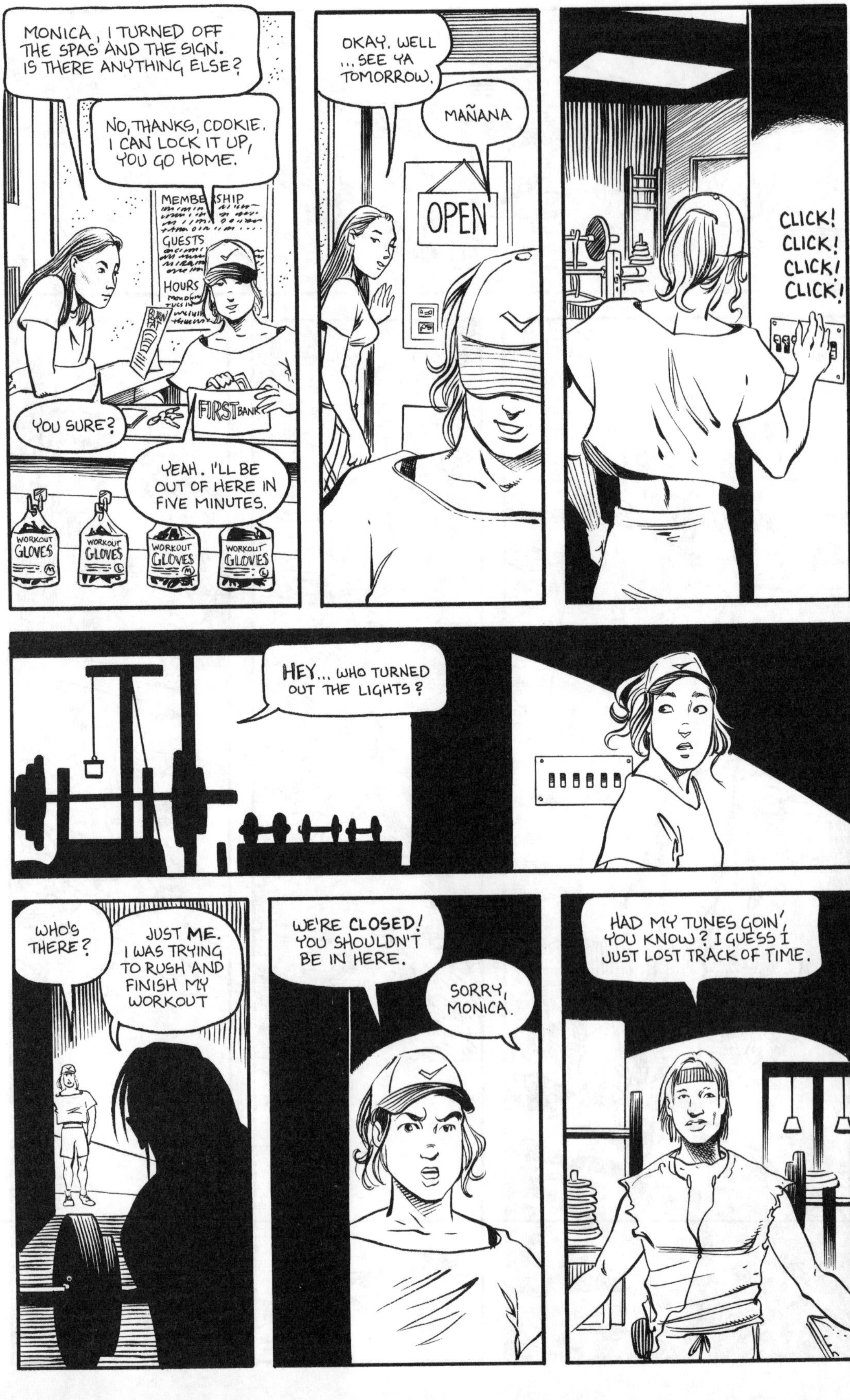
MONICA, I TURNED OFF THE SPAS AND THE SIGN. IS THERE ANYTHING ELSE?
NO, THANKS, COOKIE. I CAN LOCK IT UP, YOU GO HOME.
MEMBERSHIP
GUESTS
HOURS
BURN FAT
FIRST BANK
YOU SURE?
YEAH. I'LL BE OUT OF HERE IN FIVE MINUTES.
WORKOUT GLOVES M
WORKOUT GLOVES L
WORKOUT GLOVES M
WORKOUT GLOVES L
OKAY. WELL ...SEE YA TOMORROW.
MAÑANA
OPEN
CLICK! CLICK! CLICK! CLICK!
HEY... WHO TURNED OUT THE LIGHTS?
WHO'S THERE?
JUST ME. I WAS TRYING TO RUSH AND FINISH MY WORKOUT
WE'RE CLOSED! YOU SHOULDN'T BE IN HERE.
SORRY, MONICA.
HAD MY TUNES GOIN', YOU KNOW? I GUESS I JUST LOST TRACK OF TIME.

FBI Special Agent Sara Bryan caught the 6AM Northwest Airlines flight from Washington D.C. to Parkhaw, New York and was met by Deputy Richard Arnold of the local police. Arnold looked like he'd been dragged out of bed by a pre-dawn phone call and greeted Sara with a sullen hello. They talked little during the fifteen minute drive to the coroner's office and that suited Sara just fine. She used the time to collect her thoughts and admire the multi-colored woods of upper state New York as they wound their way through the sleepy town of Parkhaw, population 1,650. Downtown was small but cute in that deliberate architecturally restored sort of way. Tree lined streets and clapboard houses offered a sentimental feeling of yesterlife while elaborate country estates hid in the surrounding woods on some of the most expensive real estate in the country. Fortune 500 CEOs and reclusive celebrities drove into town daily for milk and farm fresh eggs, pretending to be locals in their Eddie Bauer jackets and $150 blue jeans. Sara had noticed numerous private jets parked to one side of the airport when she landed. Must be nice, she mused.

The Parkhaw County Coroner's office was housed in a pleasant, single story brick building that could have passed for a dentist office if not for the sign out front. Several police cruisers and the van of a local television station were parked on the pebble parking lot and people lingered around the entrance to the building, held at bay by another one of Parkhaw's finest, looking no more awake than Deputy Arnold. Sara followed her man into the building and waited irritably in the front room with two state troopers drinking coffee while someone went to find the chief of police. The sound of a commode flushing was heard down the hallway. A minute later a tall man with a hawk-like face walked into the room, offered her a clammy handshake and introduced himself as Tom Schtickmann, Chief of Police.

"I suppose you've been briefed on the situation," he said as he led her down the hall.

"Yes, but I'd still like to hear it from you," she replied.

They turned a corner and walked through an open door into the coroner's examination room. The room was small and stark white. A bald, middle-aged man in green scrubs leaned against a steel examining table and wrote on a legal sized form held in a clipboard while two grim faced men in suits whispered to each other off to one side. Sara was introduced to the coroner and the two men, who turned out to be the mayor and his son-in-law, the deputy mayor. The mayor shook his head. "Never, never has anything like this happened here before. Never. It's a black day in Parkhaw."

"Yes sir," Sara agreed. "May I see the head?"

The coroner moved to one side. Laid out on the table behind him were three items: a triangular bone about 4 inches across, a large bone about 18 inches long and a skull with the lower jaw intact. The triangular bone had a hole near the middle large enough for Sara to stick her finger through.

"The skull was found yesterday in a gully in the woods, about twenty miles from here," Schtickmann said. "We turned up the scapula and femur this morning during a sweep of the area. They were within forty yards of where we found the skull."

Sara leaned closer to examine the skull. "No sign of injury. Teeth intact. Looks female."

"It is. The other bones, too," the coroner said. "I sent samples to the bureau last night along with a dental mold. They'll be able to test to see if the bones belong to the same body. I suspect they do. Judging from the size of these pieces, I'd say she was a little over five feet tall, a hundred and twenty pounds or so."

"Hmm" Sara nodded. The beeper buzzed on her belt. She checked the number; it was Keith Rankin. She excused herself and went into the hall to return his call.

"Rankin."

"It's Sara Bryan, sir."

"We have a match on the dental mold."

"That's fast."

"It doesn't take long when the subject's been in a federal prison."

"So, who do we have here?"

"You ready for this? It's Veronica Bouedaue."

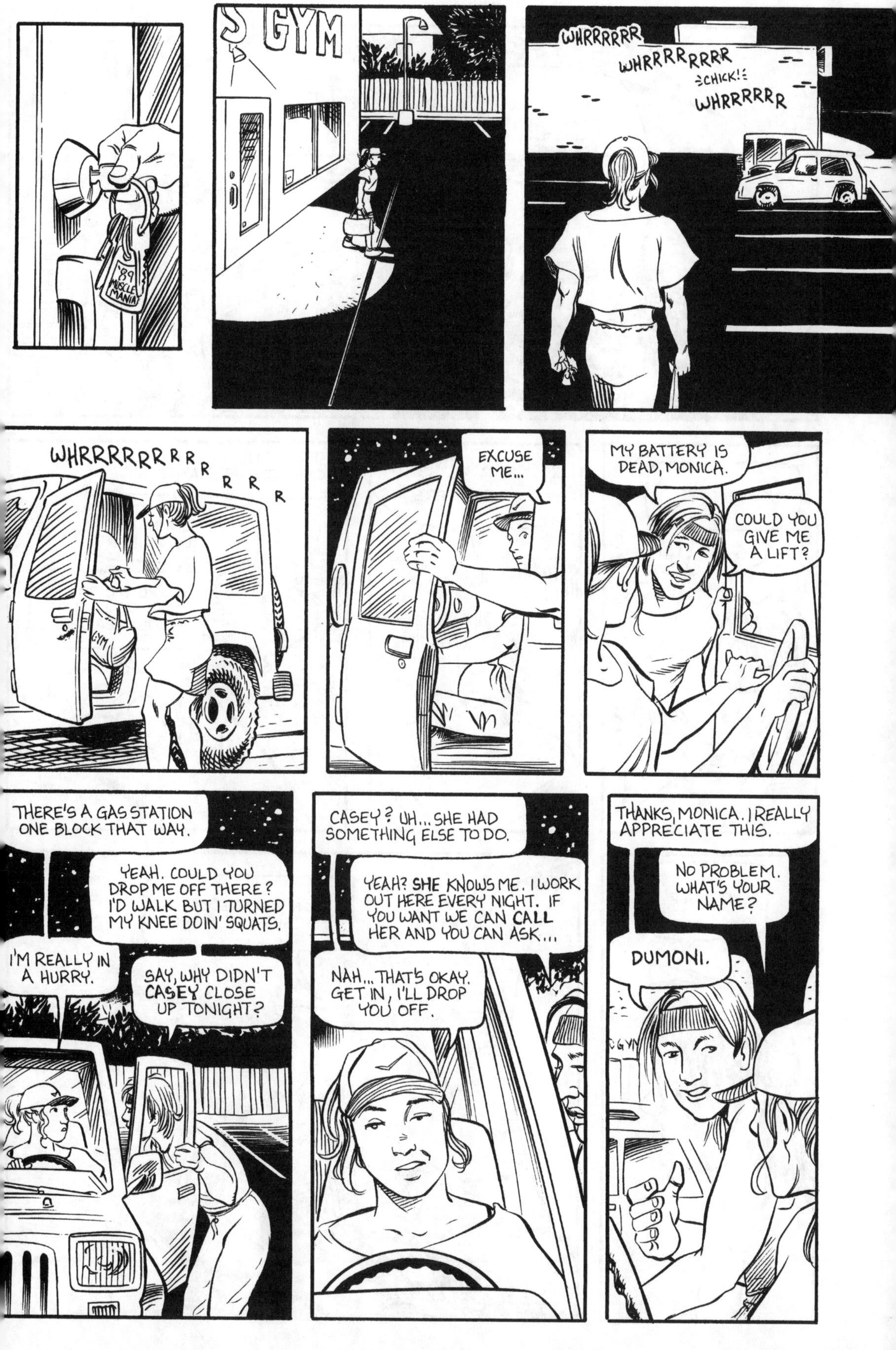
'89 MUSCLE MANIA
S GYM
WHRRRRRR
WHRRRRRRRR
CHICK!
WHRRRRRR
WHRRRRRRRRRRR
GYM
EXCUSE ME...
MY BATTERY IS DEAD, MONICA.
COULD YOU GIVE ME A LIFT?
THERE'S A GAS STATION ONE BLOCK THAT WAY.
YEAH. COULD YOU DROP ME OFF THERE? I'D WALK BUT I TURNED MY KNEE DOIN' SQUATS.
I'M REALLY IN A HURRY.
SAY, WHY DIDN'T CASEY CLOSE UP TONIGHT?
CASEY? UH... SHE HAD SOMETHING ELSE TO DO.
YEAH? SHE KNOWS ME. I WORK OUT HERE EVERY NIGHT. IF YOU WANT WE CAN CALL HER AND YOU CAN ASK...
NAH... THAT'S OKAY. GET IN, I'LL DROP YOU OFF.
THANKS, MONICA. I REALLY APPRECIATE THIS.
NO PROBLEM. WHAT'S YOUR NAME?
DUMONI.

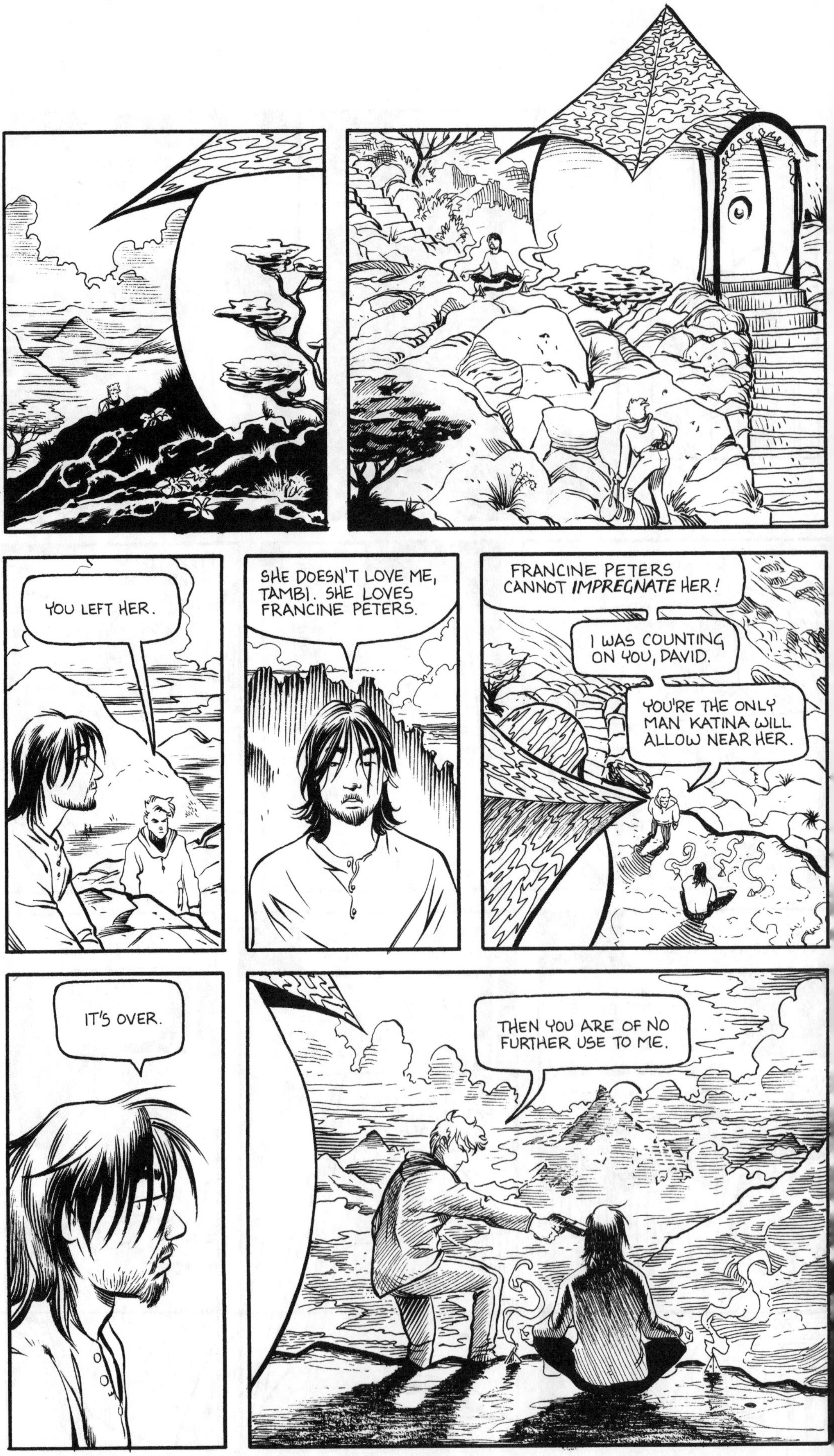
YOU LEFT HER.
SHE DOESN'T LOVE ME, TAMBI. SHE LOVES FRANCINE PETERS.
FRANCINE PETERS CANNOT IMPREGNATE HER!
I WAS COUNTING ON YOU, DAVID.
YOU'RE THE ONLY MAN KATINA WILL ALLOW NEAR HER.
IT'S OVER.
THEN YOU ARE OF NO FURTHER USE TO ME.

Somewhere, over the rainbow,
Way up high,
There's a land that I heard of
Once in a lullaby.

Somewhere, over the rainbow,
Skies are blue,
And the dreams that you dare to dream
Really do come true.

Somewhere Over The Rainbow lyrics by E. Y. Harburg

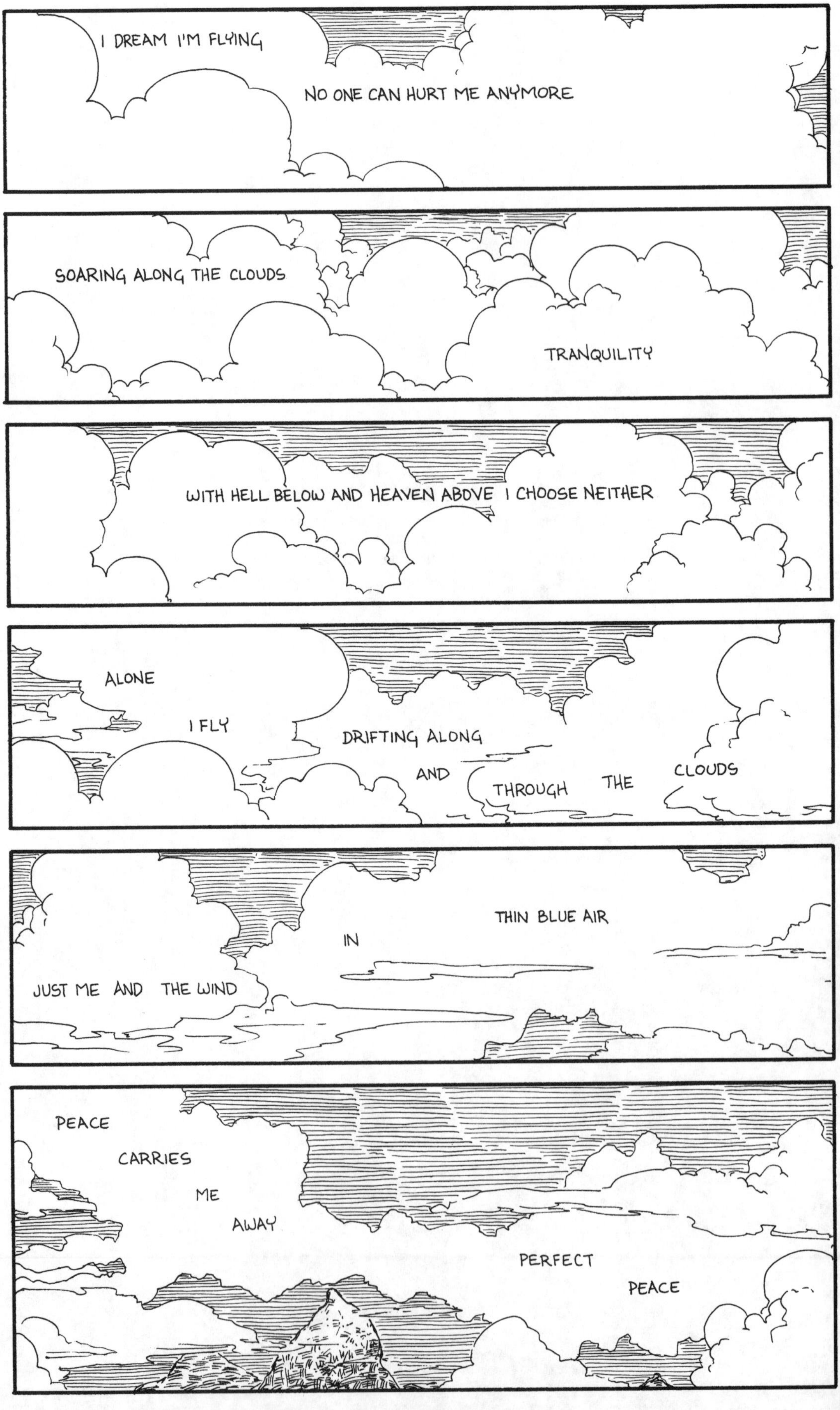
I DREAM I'M FLYING
NO ONE CAN HURT ME ANYMORE
SOARING ALONG THE CLOUDS
TRANQUILITY
WITH HELL BELOW AND HEAVEN ABOVE I CHOOSE NEITHER
ALONE
I FLY
DRIFTING ALONG
AND
THROUGH
THE
CLOUDS
JUST ME AND THE WIND
IN
THIN BLUE AIR
PEACE
CARRIES
ME
AWAY
PERFECT
PEACE

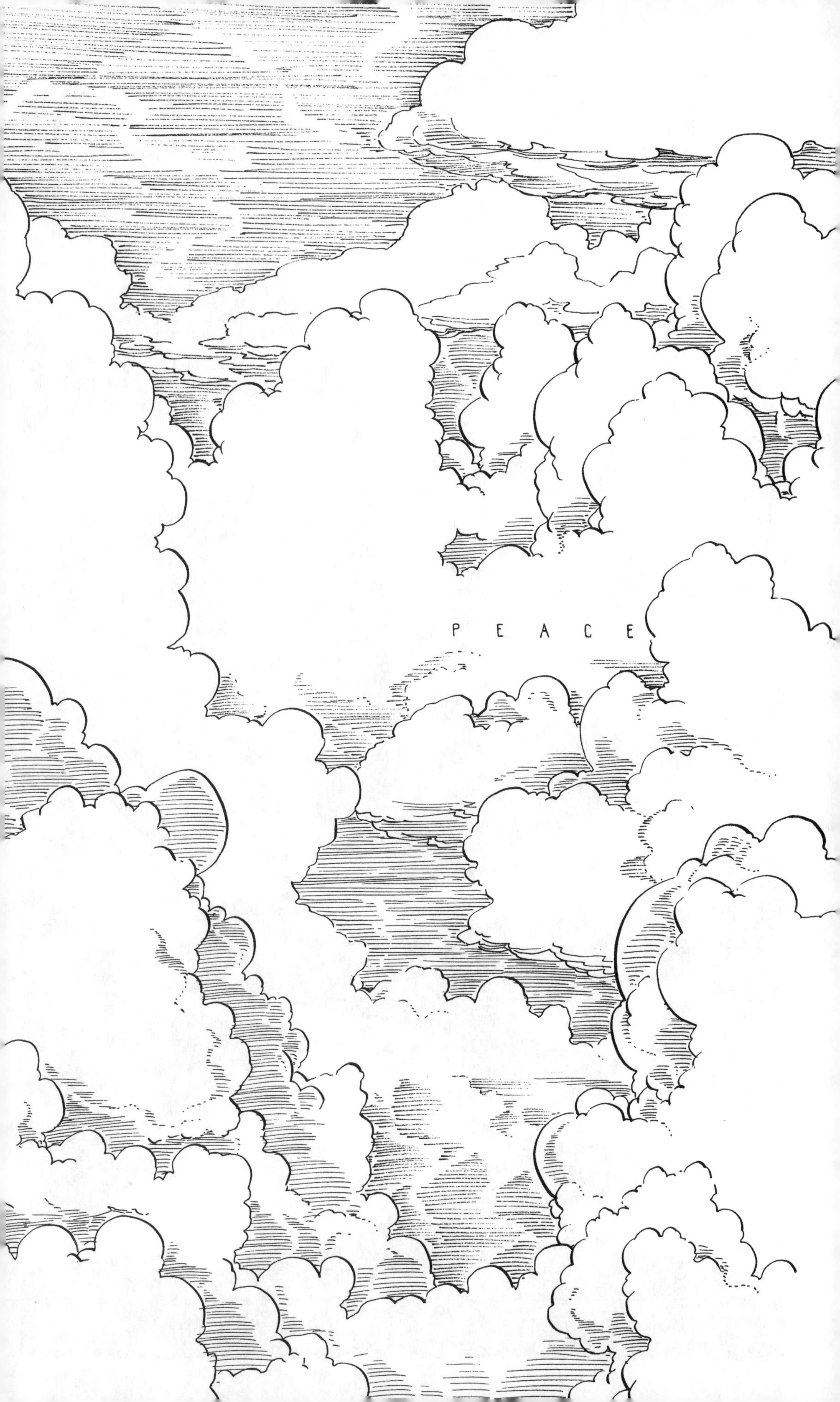
PEACE

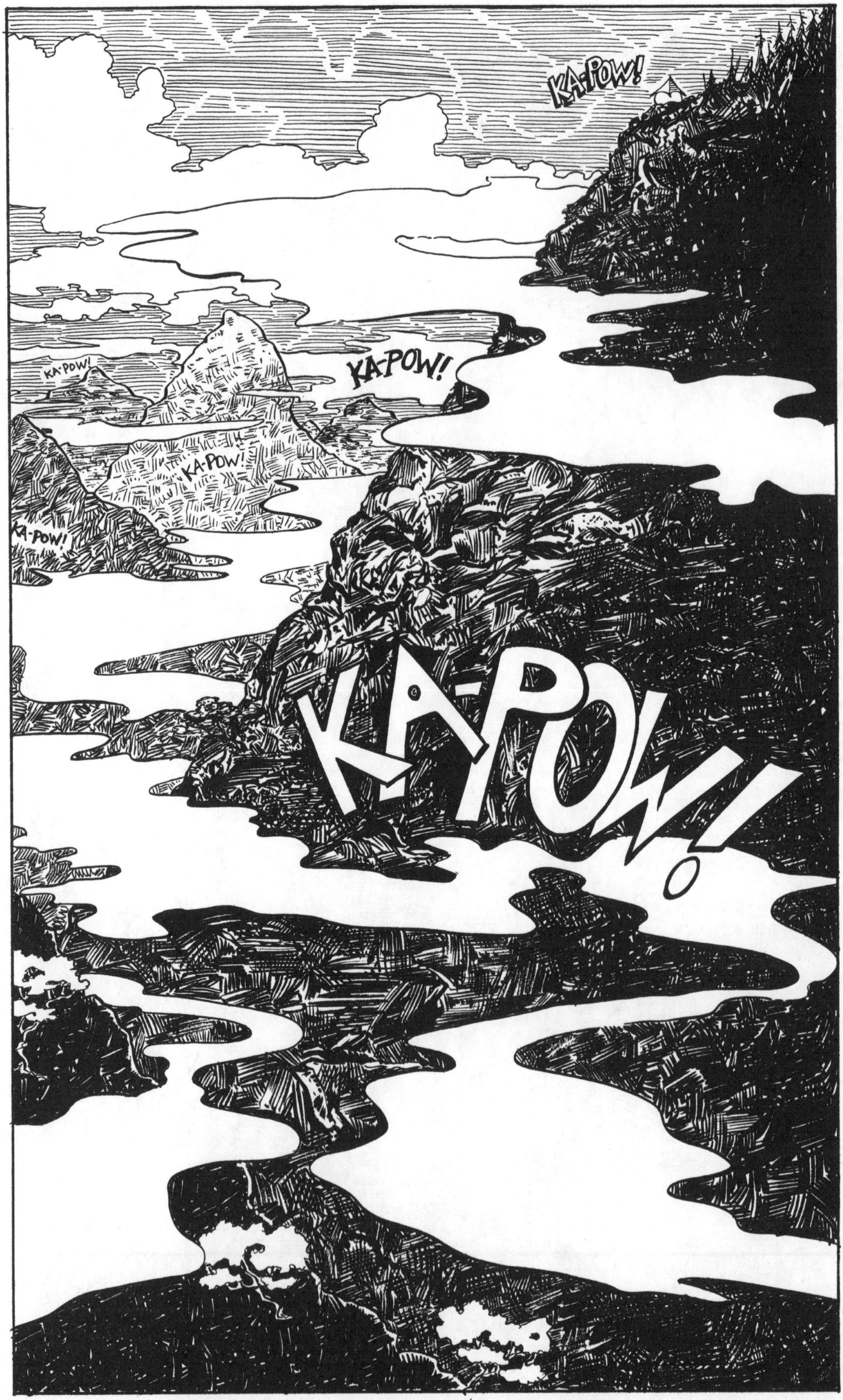
KA-POW!
KA-POW!
KA-POW!
KA-POW!
KA-POW!
KA-POW!

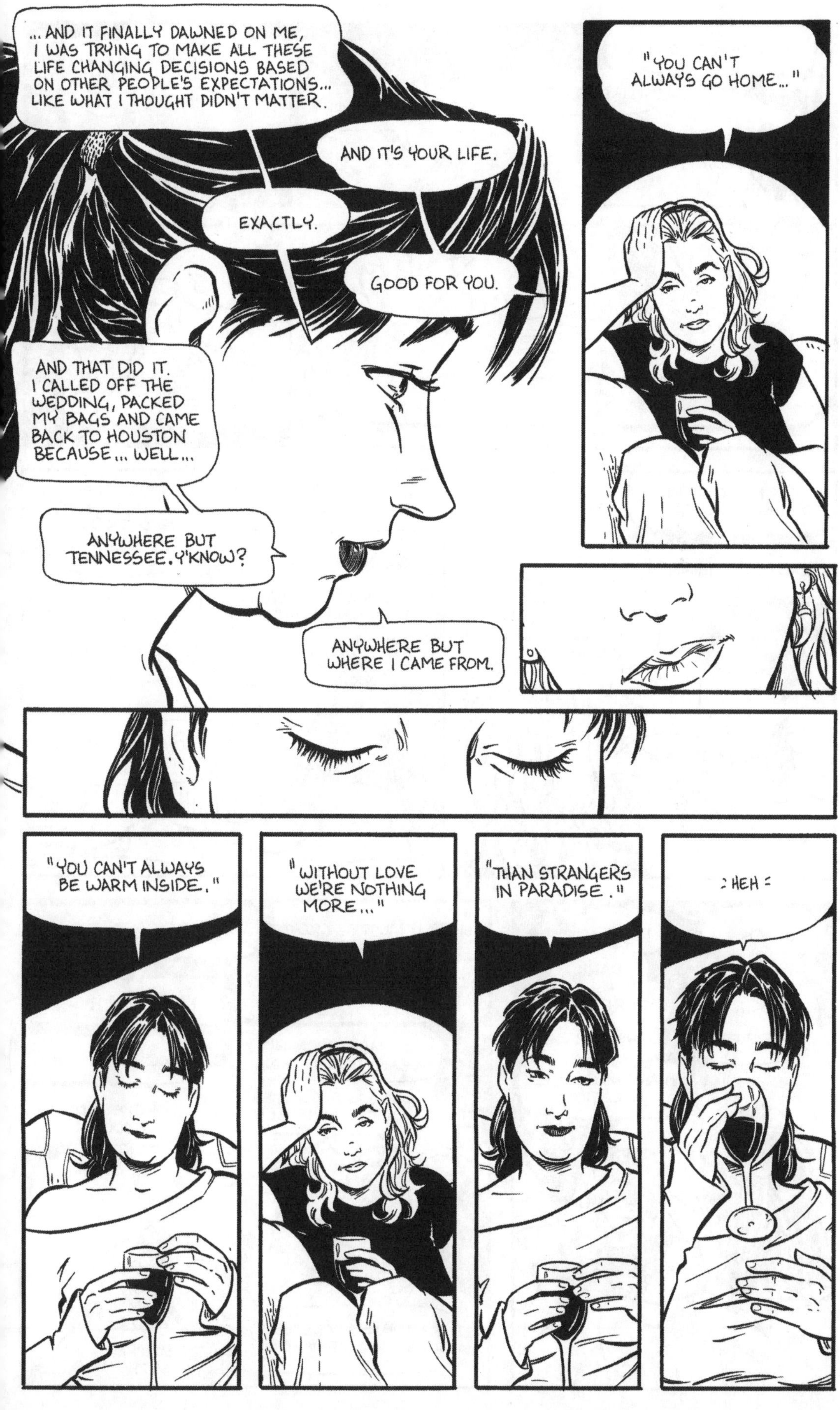

... AND IT FINALLY DAWNED ON ME, I WAS TRYING TO MAKE ALL THESE LIFE CHANGING DECISIONS BASED ON OTHER PEOPLE'S EXPECTATIONS... LIKE WHAT I THOUGHT DIDN'T MATTER.
AND IT'S YOUR LIFE.
EXACTLY.
GOOD FOR YOU.
AND THAT DID IT. I CALLED OFF THE WEDDING, PACKED MY BAGS AND CAME BACK TO HOUSTON BECAUSE... WELL...
ANYWHERE BUT TENNESSEE. Y'KNOW?
ANYWHERE BUT WHERE I CAME FROM.
"YOU CAN'T ALWAYS GO HOME..."
"YOU CAN'T ALWAYS BE WARM INSIDE."
"WITHOUT LOVE WE'RE NOTHING MORE..."
"THAN STRANGERS IN PARADISE."
:HEH:

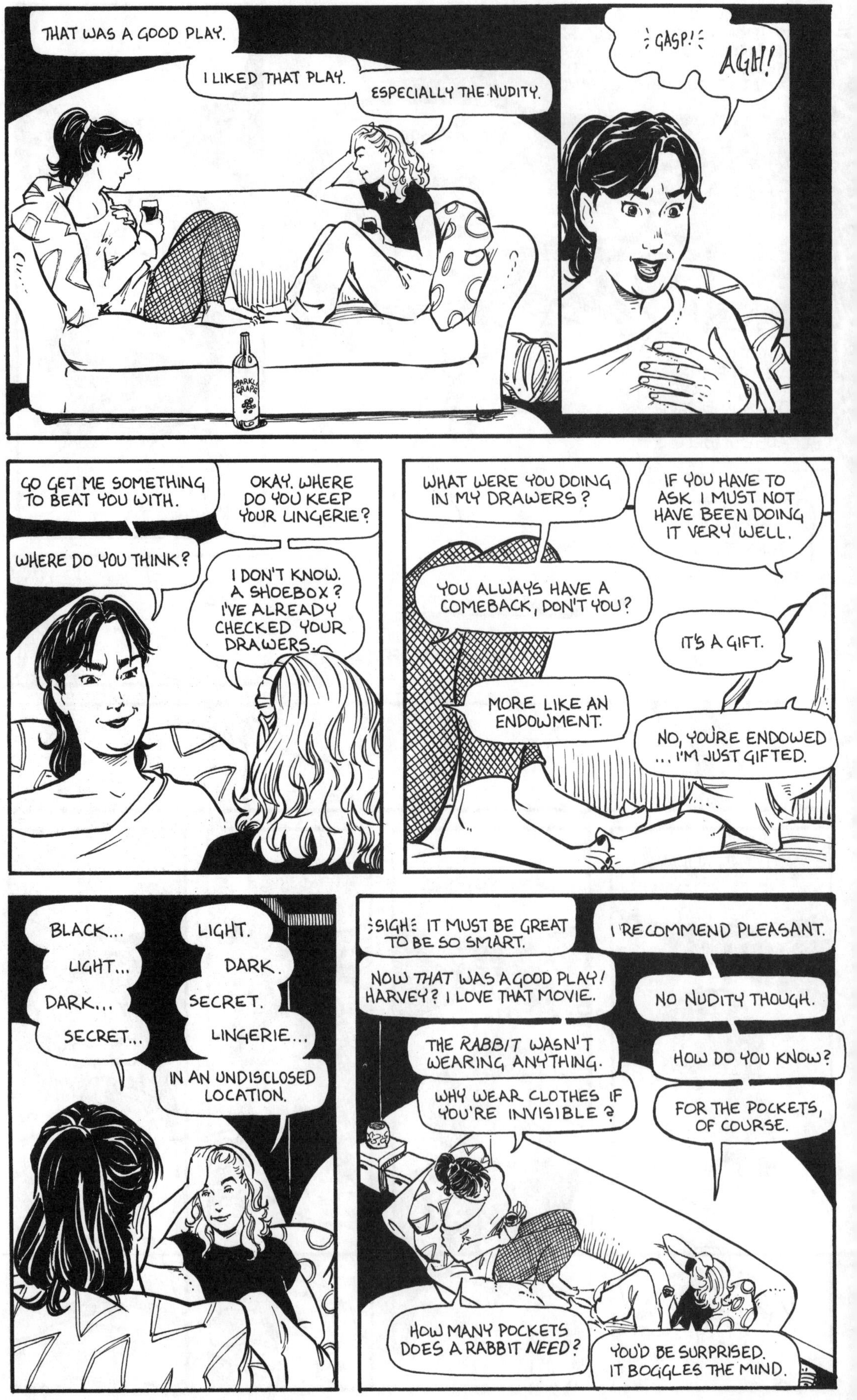
THAT WAS A GOOD PLAY.
I LIKED THAT PLAY.
ESPECIALLY THE NUDITY.
GASP!
AGH!
GO GET ME SOMETHING TO BEAT YOU WITH.
OKAY. WHERE DO YOU KEEP YOUR LINGERIE?
WHERE DO YOU THINK?
I DON'T KNOW. A SHOEBOX? I'VE ALREADY CHECKED YOUR DRAWERS.
WHAT WERE YOU DOING IN MY DRAWERS?
IF YOU HAVE TO ASK I MUST NOT HAVE BEEN DOING IT VERY WELL.
YOU ALWAYS HAVE A COMEBACK, DON'T YOU?
IT'S A GIFT.
MORE LIKE AN ENDOWMENT.
NO, YOU'RE ENDOWED ... I'M JUST GIFTED.
BLACK...
LIGHT...
DARK...
SECRET...
LIGHT.
DARK.
SECRET.
LINGERIE...
IN AN UNDISCLOSED LOCATION.
SIGH IT MUST BE GREAT TO BE SO SMART.
I RECOMMEND PLEASANT.
NOW THAT WAS A GOOD PLAY! HARVEY? I LOVE THAT MOVIE.
NO NUDITY THOUGH.
THE RABBIT WASN'T WEARING ANYTHING.
HOW DO YOU KNOW?
WHY WEAR CLOTHES IF YOU'RE INVISIBLE?
FOR THE POCKETS, OF COURSE.
SPARKLING GRAPE
HOW MANY POCKETS DOES A RABBIT NEED?
YOU'D BE SURPRISED. IT BOGGLES THE MIND.

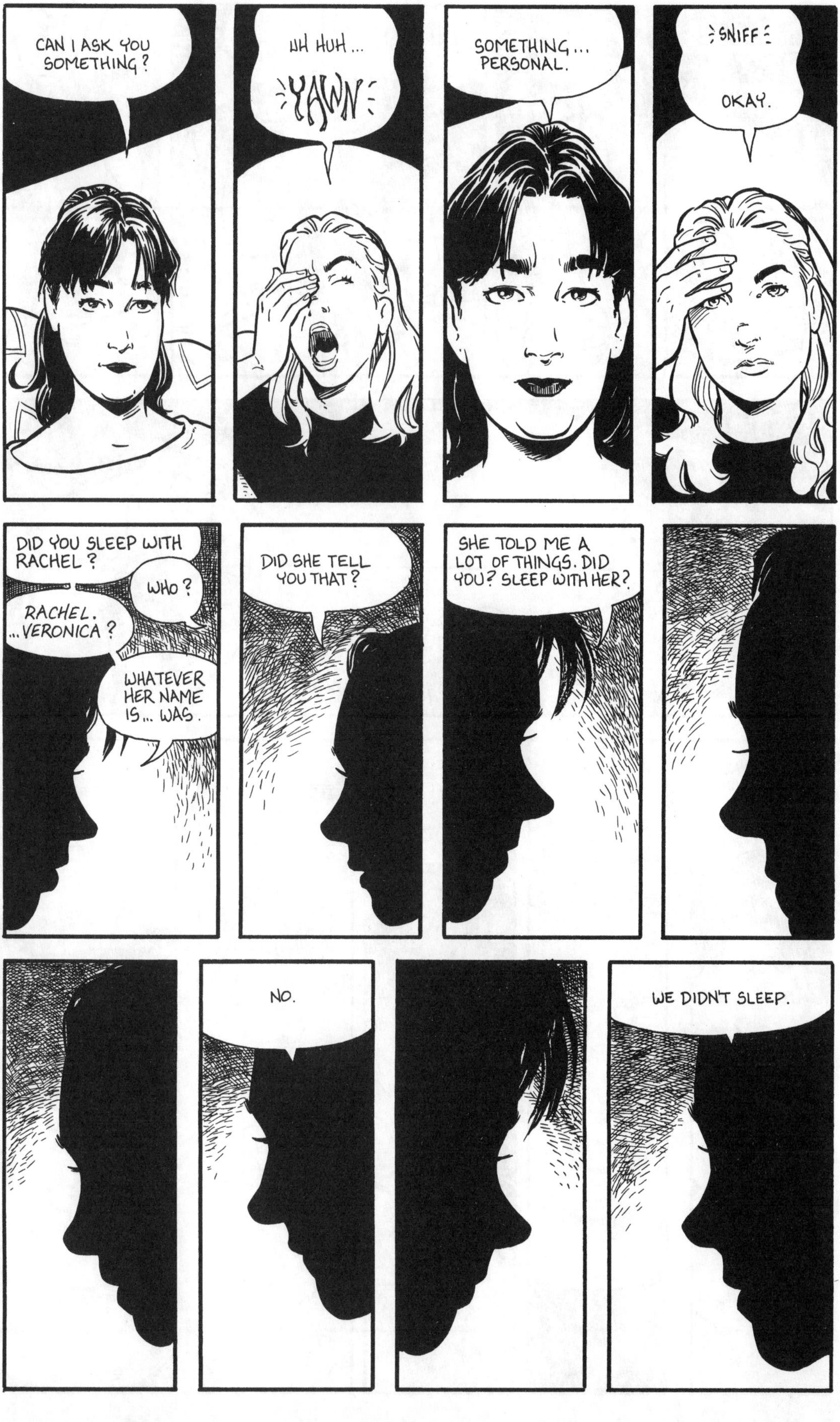
CAN I ASK YOU SOMETHING?
UH HUH...
YAWN
SOMETHING... PERSONAL.
SNIFF
OKAY.
DID YOU SLEEP WITH RACHEL?
WHO?
RACHEL. ...VERONICA?
WHATEVER HER NAME IS... WAS.
DID SHE TELL YOU THAT?
SHE TOLD ME A LOT OF THINGS. DID YOU? SLEEP WITH HER?
NO.
WE DIDN'T SLEEP.

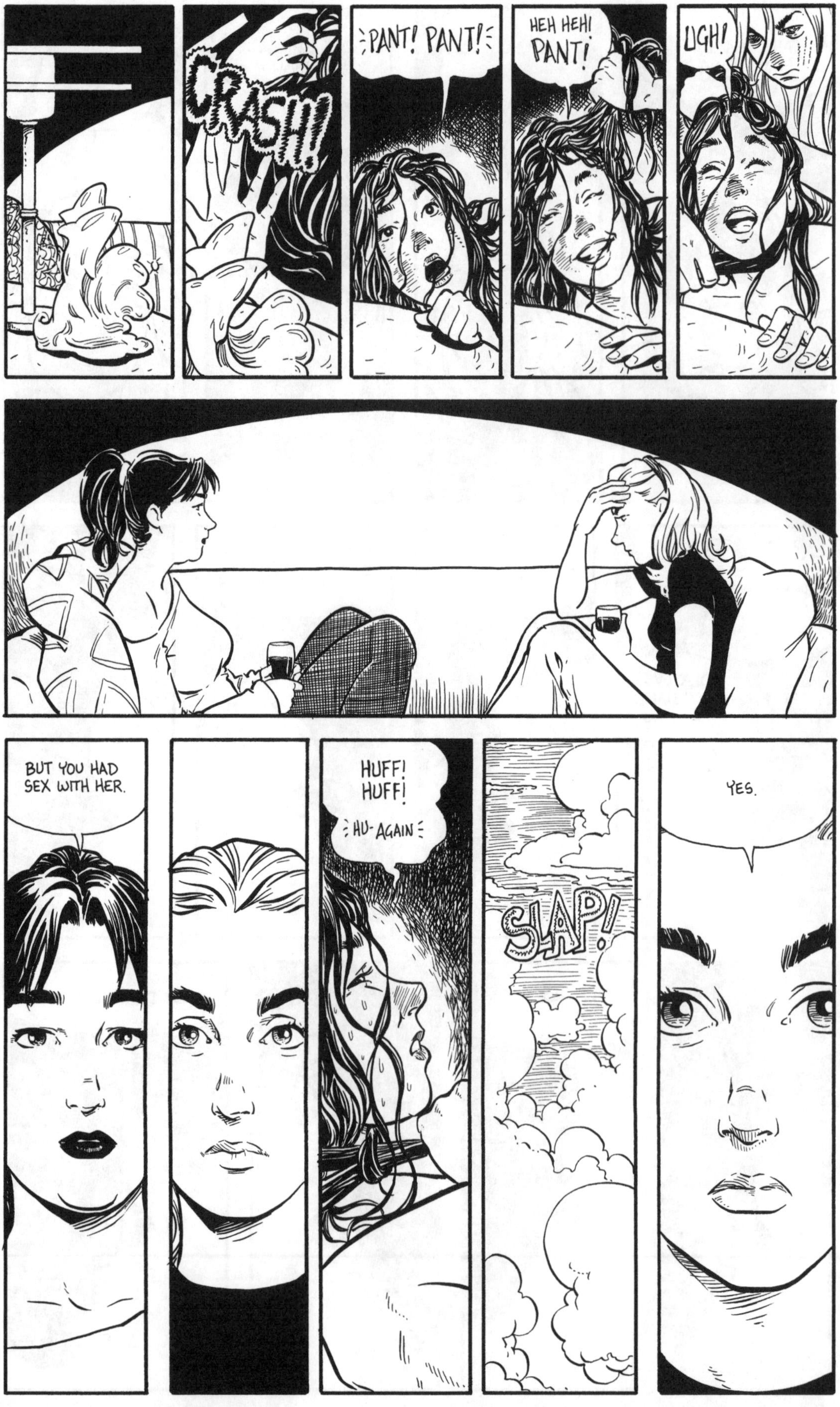

CRASH!
PANT! PANT!
HEH HEH! PANT!
UGH!
BUT YOU HAD SEX WITH HER.
HUFF! HUFF!
HU-AGAIN
SLAP!
YES.

Just a smile
Just a glance
The Prince of Darkness
He just walked past.

-Roy Buchanan

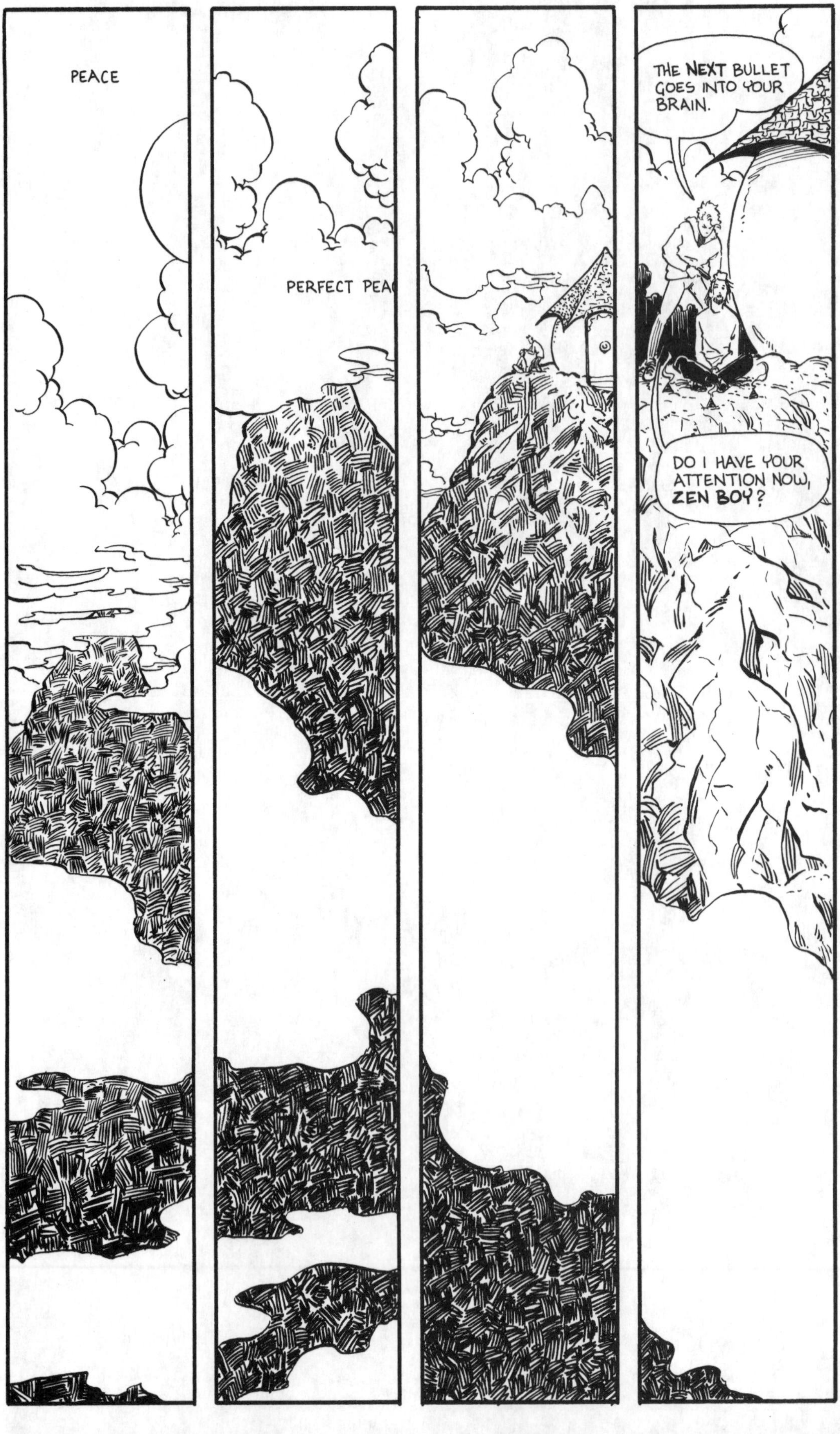
PEACE
PERFECT PEAC
THE NEXT BULLET GOES INTO YOUR BRAIN.
DO I HAVE YOUR ATTENTION NOW, ZEN BOY?

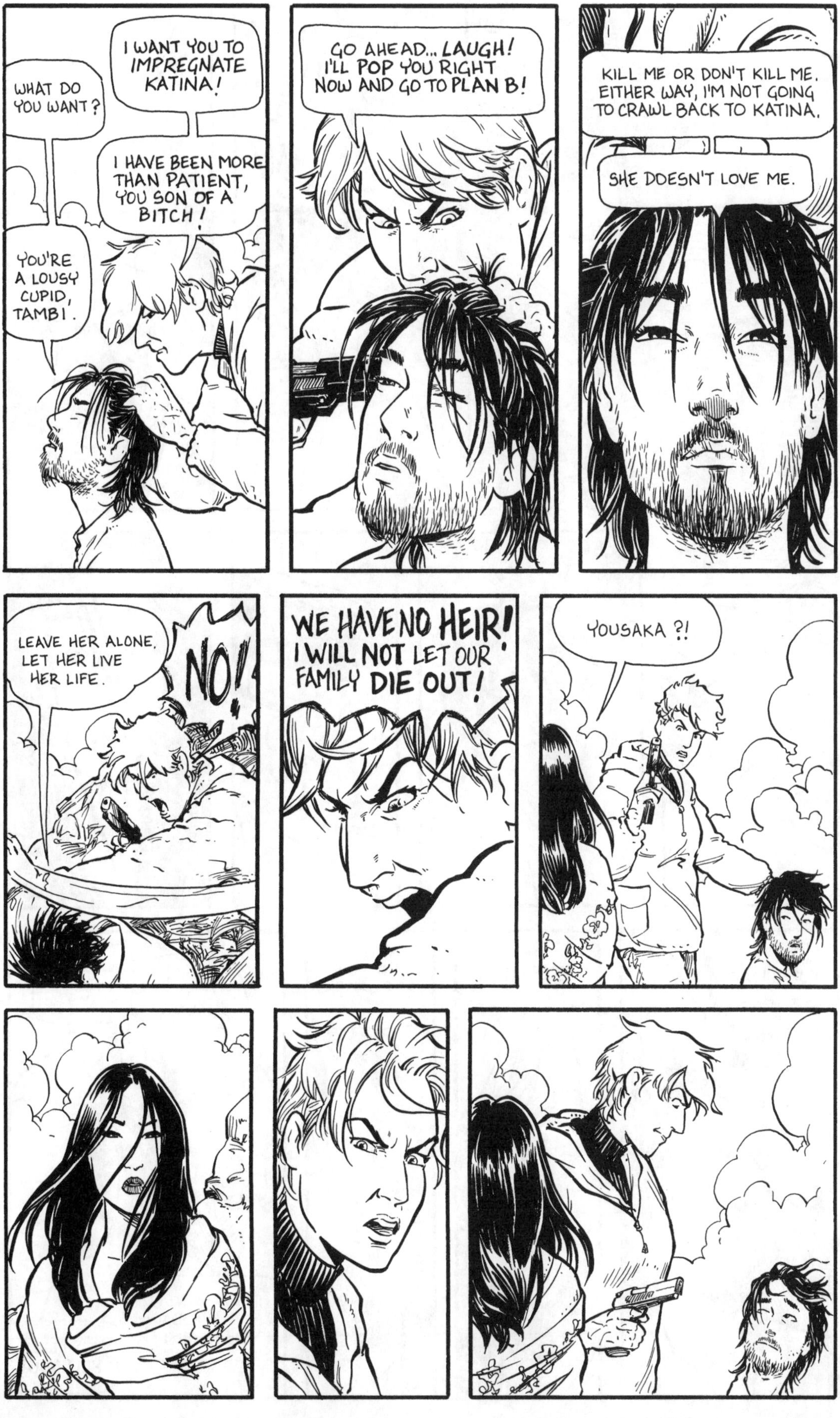
WHAT DO YOU WANT?
I WANT YOU TO IMPREGNATE KATINA!
I HAVE BEEN MORE THAN PATIENT, YOU SON OF A BITCH!
YOU'RE A LOUSY CUPID, TAMBI.
GO AHEAD... LAUGH! I'LL POP YOU RIGHT NOW AND GO TO PLAN B!
KILL ME OR DON'T KILL ME. EITHER WAY, I'M NOT GOING TO CRAWL BACK TO KATINA.
SHE DOESN'T LOVE ME.
LEAVE HER ALONE. LET HER LIVE HER LIFE.
NO!
WE HAVE NO HEIR! I WILL NOT LET OUR FAMILY DIE OUT!
YOUSAKA ?!

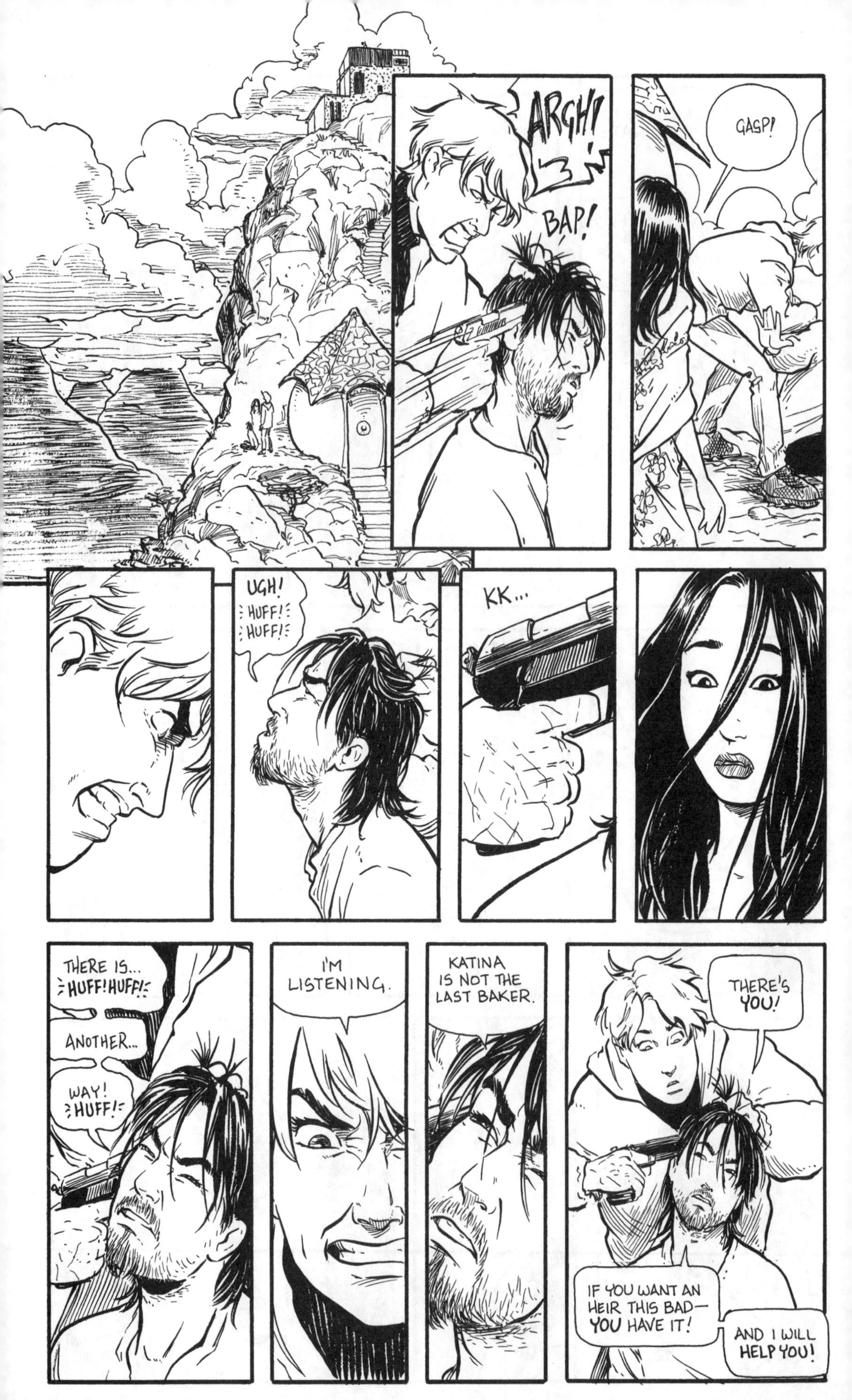
ARGH!
BAP!
GASP!
UGH!
HUFF! HUFF!
KK...
THERE IS...
HUFF! HUFF!
ANOTHER...
WAY! HUFF!
I'M LISTENING.
KATINA IS NOT THE LAST BAKER.
THERE'S YOU!
IF YOU WANT AN HEIR THIS BAD— YOU HAVE IT!
AND I WILL HELP YOU!

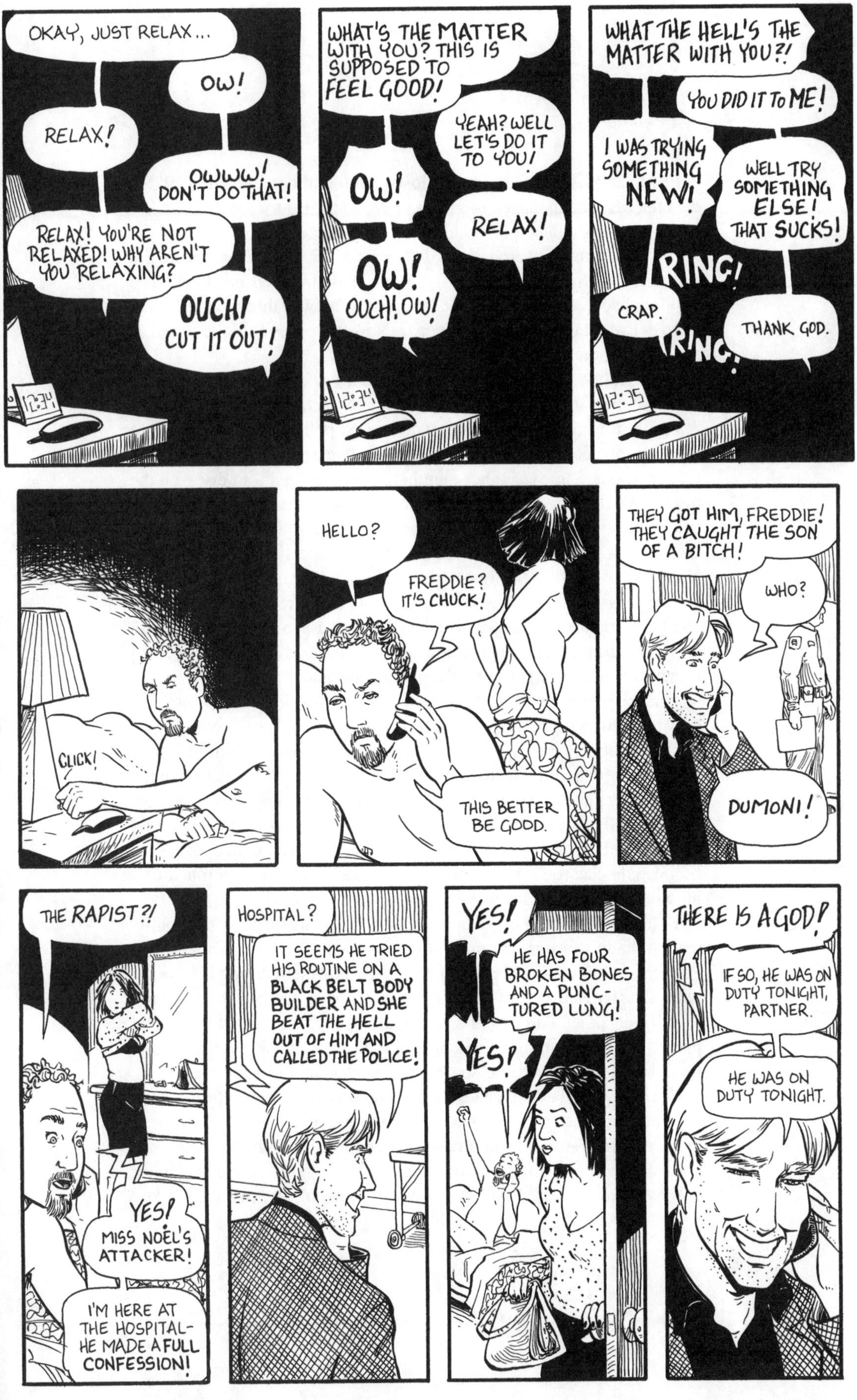

OKAY, JUST RELAX...
OW!
RELAX!
OWWW! DON'T DO THAT!
RELAX! YOU'RE NOT RELAXED! WHY AREN'T YOU RELAXING?
OUCH! CUT IT OUT!
12:34
WHAT'S THE MATTER WITH YOU? THIS IS SUPPOSED TO FEEL GOOD!
YEAH? WELL LET'S DO IT TO YOU!
OW!
RELAX!
OW! OUCH! OW!
12:34
WHAT THE HELL'S THE MATTER WITH YOU?!
YOU DID IT TO ME!
I WAS TRYING SOMETHING NEW!
WELL TRY SOMETHING ELSE! THAT SUCKS!
RING!
CRAP.
RING!
THANK GOD.
12:35
CLICK!
HELLO?
FREDDIE? IT'S CHUCK!
THIS BETTER BE GOOD.
THEY GOT HIM, FREDDIE! THEY CAUGHT THE SON OF A BITCH!
WHO?
DUMONI!
THE RAPIST?!
YES! MISS NOËL'S ATTACKER!
I'M HERE AT THE HOSPITAL- HE MADE A FULL CONFESSION!
HOSPITAL?
IT SEEMS HE TRIED HIS ROUTINE ON A BLACK BELT BODY BUILDER AND SHE BEAT THE HELL OUT OF HIM AND CALLED THE POLICE!
YES!
HE HAS FOUR BROKEN BONES AND A PUNCTURED LUNG!
YES!
THERE IS A GOD!
IF SO, HE WAS ON DUTY TONIGHT, PARTNER.
HE WAS ON DUTY TONIGHT.

FBI Special Agent Sara Bryan closed the file folder containing all the data the FBI had managed to gather on Veronica Bouedaue over the last eight years and pushed her chair away from the desk. She checked the big G-Shock plastic watch on her left wrist: 1:45 A.M. Crap, where did the time go? Sara sighed heavily, stood and stretched her back. The building had been full when she sat down to browse through the folder, hand delivered from Janine in records. Now there was only the sound of the cleaning crew a few doors away.

Sara grabbed her empty coffee mug and walked down the hall to a small kitchenette tucked in the wall like a New Mexico cave dwelling. She said hi to the cleaning lady who smiled politely over the noise of the vacuum cleaner and continued wiping the glass windows of the conference room. Sara rinsed her mug in the sink and put it to dry with the others on a dishtowel spread on the counter. A wave of exhaustion made her pause a moment and stare blankly at the drain. "Time to go home," she thought. It had been over twenty hours since she'd flown to New York at 5 A.M. to investigate the discovery of a human skull in the woods outside a small town. Forensic tests had already confirmed the identity through dental records in the FBI database. Since the victim had served time in a federal penitentiary, the match had taken less than ten minutes. It was a Parker Girl: Veronica Bouedaue.

Parker Girls were a rare find for the bureau. Beside Miss Bouedaue, only two others had surfaced in nine years; one was discovered last year by a sanitation worker in New York's harbor district, stuffed into a dumpster with her throat slit. The other girl had been thrown through the triple safety glass of a high-rise apartment in Hong Kong four years ago. She fell fifty-three stories onto the roof of a dance club, smashing through with a ton of debris onto the disc jockey. The police arrived to find people cheering. Apparently the new jock had not been much of a hit with demanding patrons.

Both girls had been on a short list of Parker Girl suspects but confirmation hadn't occurred until after their deaths when Tony "Tip" Palmerra, a hit man for Sal Tucciani, mentioned them during interviews with the bureau before entering the witness protection program. Identifying other Parker Girls and building a case against them had proven to be a frustrating challenge for the bureau, made even more difficult by an element of fear shared by their aphonic victims.

The Parker Girls were deadly social spies, women who infiltrated the lives of prominent men and women in power and controlled them from the bedroom. Veronica had almost made it into the White House until her cover was blown by an article in the D.C. Daily. A former Parker Girl going by the alias "Miracle" broke the code of silence and gave key evidence to Marshal Weinstein, a staff reporter known for his editorials on the mythic world-power group, The Big Six. Weinstein's exposé led to the arrest of Veronica Bouedaue, then posing as Beverly Pace, fiancée to Senator Robert Henneman, the leading presidential candidate. The morning the story broke, Darcy Parker herself was found dead of an apparent self-inflicted gunshot wound in the bedroom of her Bel-Air mansion.

Weinstein had refused to reveal the identity of his "Miracle" source to the FBI, which was preparing charges against him for withholding evidence when he was found brutally murdered in his Washington, D.C. apartment. He had been dismembered alive; his fingers cut off one by one, then his hands. He bled to death, tied to a kitchen chair. His apartment had been ransacked. The hard drive of his computer and most of his paper records had been taken. His killer, or killers, had never been caught.

Nobody knew where a Parker Girl was at any given moment, but you could tell where they'd been by the trail of death and violence they left behind them. Now, one by one, the Parker Girls themselves were meeting a similar fate.

Sara walked back to her office, picked up her purse and coat, locked the door and rode the elevator down to the parking garage. One thing seemed certain, Sara thought as she walked to her car, somebody was finding Parker Girls and killing them one by one. Whether it was an enemy or in-house discipline, she didn't know. Except for Mrs. Parker herself, the bodies had been too badly disfigured or, in the case of Veronica, dismembered and left to rot in the woods. Whoever was behind the deaths was a consummate professional, leaving no trace evidence behind.

Sara pulled her black BMW M3 up to the gate and, as a matter of protocol, flashed her card to Sam, the night watchman. The big steel gate slid open and Sam waved goodnight as Sara pulled out into the traffic of D.C. nightlife. She cut through several quiet side streets using precise spurts of brute power from the 333 horsepower engine before turning onto Pennsylvania Avenue to blend in with the cabs and limos working their way north.

Somewhere out there was a predator more deadly than a Parker Girl, someone who chopped their pretty little heads off and threw them out the windows of high-rise buildings. If it took the rest of her life, Sara Bryan was going to find this predator and bring him, or her, to justice. But not tonight. Tonight she would sleep. Tomorrow she would rise and do what the FBI had trained her to do: become the predator's worst enemy.

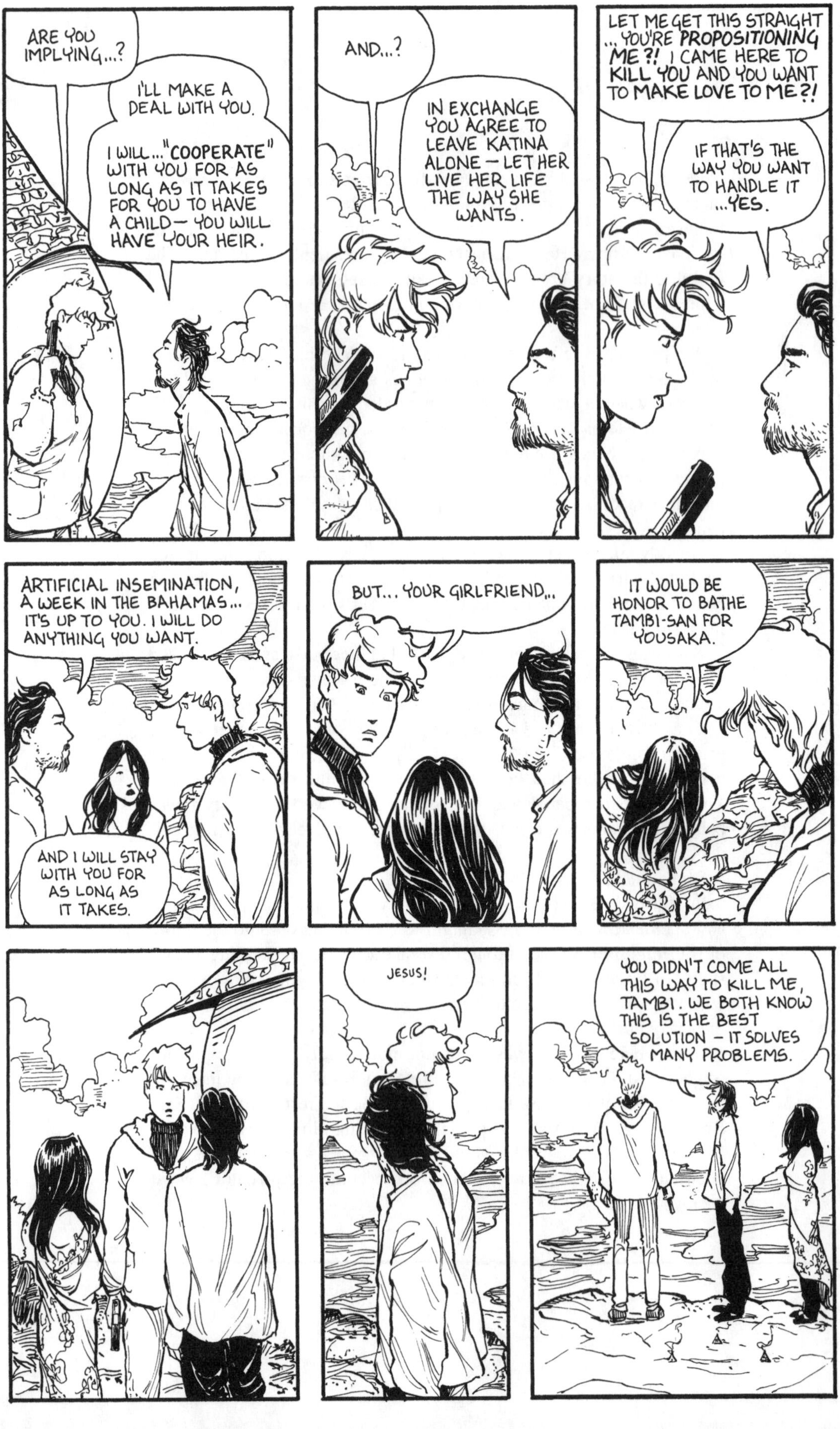
ARE YOU IMPLYING...?
I'LL MAKE A DEAL WITH YOU.
I WILL..."COOPERATE" WITH YOU FOR AS LONG AS IT TAKES FOR YOU TO HAVE A CHILD— YOU WILL HAVE YOUR HEIR.
AND...?
IN EXCHANGE YOU AGREE TO LEAVE KATINA ALONE — LET HER LIVE HER LIFE THE WAY SHE WANTS.
LET ME GET THIS STRAIGHT ...YOU'RE PROPOSITIONING ME?! I CAME HERE TO KILL YOU AND YOU WANT TO MAKE LOVE TO ME?!
IF THAT'S THE WAY YOU WANT TO HANDLE IT ...YES.
ARTIFICIAL INSEMINATION, A WEEK IN THE BAHAMAS... IT'S UP TO YOU. I WILL DO ANYTHING YOU WANT.
AND I WILL STAY WITH YOU FOR AS LONG AS IT TAKES.
BUT... YOUR GIRLFRIEND...
IT WOULD BE HONOR TO BATHE TAMBI-SAN FOR YOUSAKA.
JESUS!
YOU DIDN'T COME ALL THIS WAY TO KILL ME, TAMBI. WE BOTH KNOW THIS IS THE BEST SOLUTION – IT SOLVES MANY PROBLEMS.

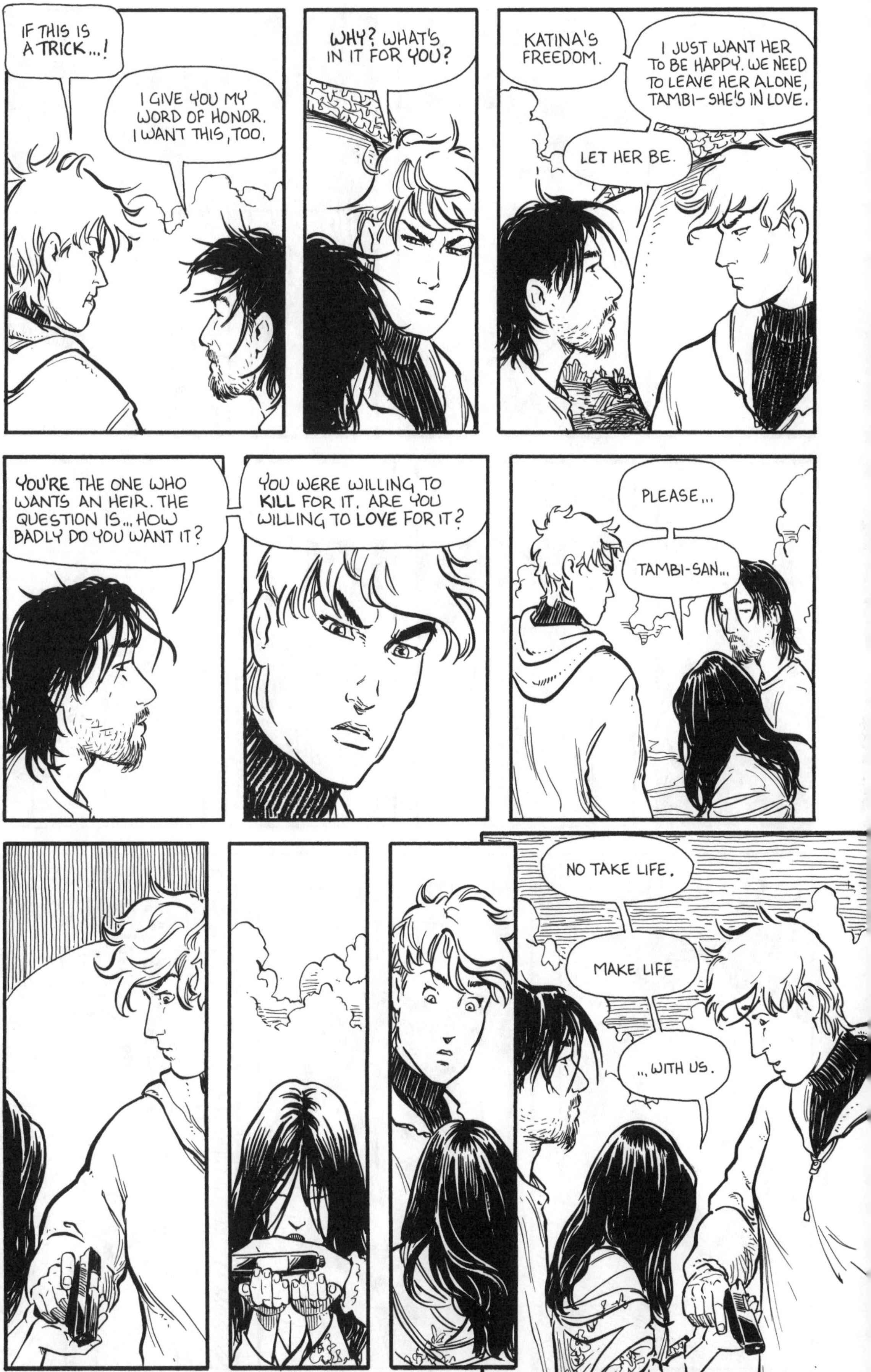
IF THIS IS A TRICK...!
I GIVE YOU MY WORD OF HONOR. I WANT THIS, TOO.
WHY? WHAT'S IN IT FOR YOU?
KATINA'S FREEDOM.
I JUST WANT HER TO BE HAPPY. WE NEED TO LEAVE HER ALONE, TAMBI– SHE'S IN LOVE.
LET HER BE.
YOU'RE THE ONE WHO WANTS AN HEIR. THE QUESTION IS... HOW BADLY DO YOU WANT IT?
YOU WERE WILLING TO KILL FOR IT. ARE YOU WILLING TO LOVE FOR IT?
PLEASE...
TAMBI-SAN...
NO TAKE LIFE.
MAKE LIFE
...WITH US.

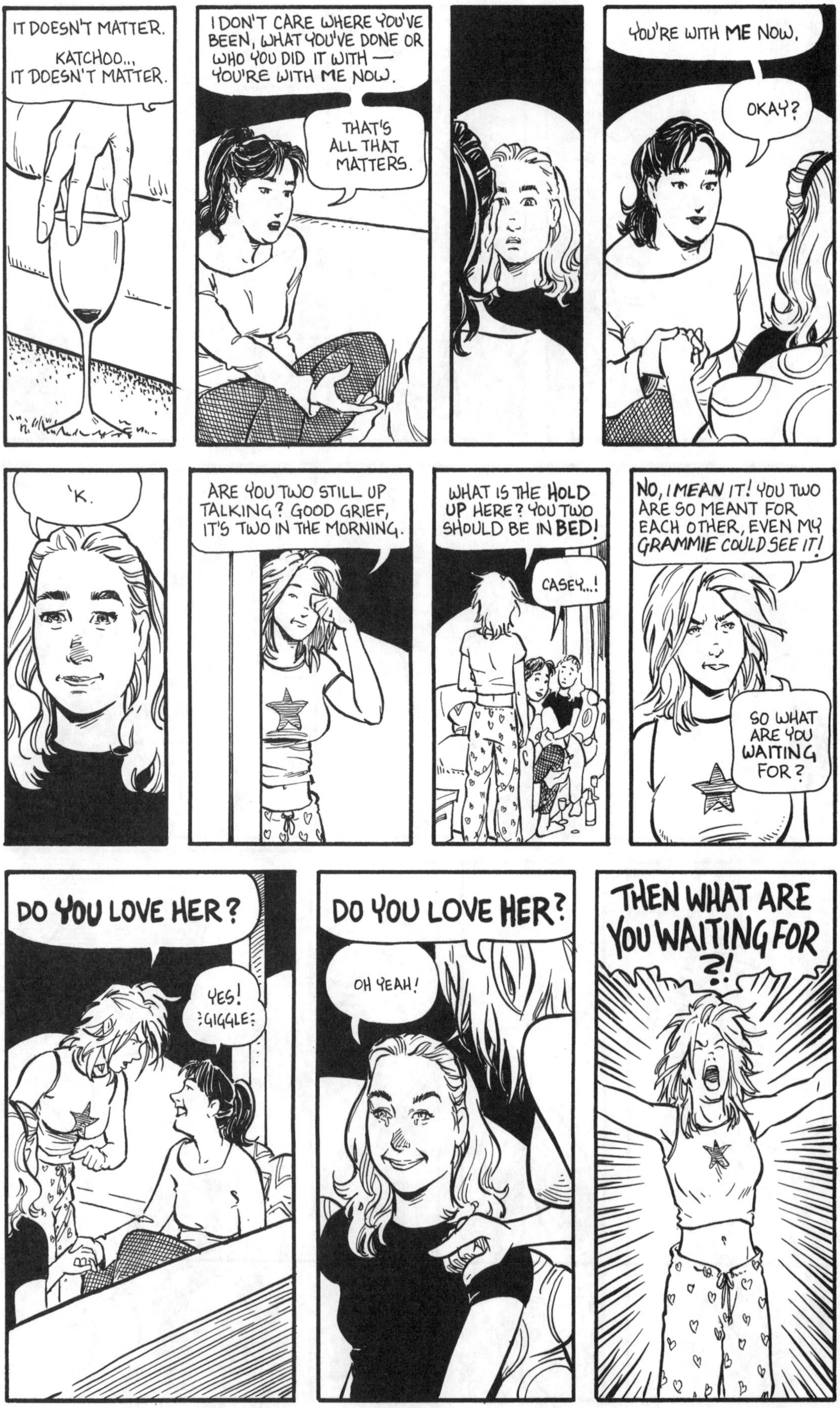
IT DOESN'T MATTER.
KATCHOO..., IT DOESN'T MATTER.
I DON'T CARE WHERE YOU'VE BEEN, WHAT YOU'VE DONE OR WHO YOU DID IT WITH — YOU'RE WITH ME NOW.
THAT'S ALL THAT MATTERS.
YOU'RE WITH ME NOW.
OKAY?
'K.
ARE YOU TWO STILL UP TALKING? GOOD GRIEF, IT'S TWO IN THE MORNING.
WHAT IS THE HOLD UP HERE? YOU TWO SHOULD BE IN BED!
CASEY...!
NO, I MEAN IT! YOU TWO ARE SO MEANT FOR EACH OTHER, EVEN MY GRAMMIE COULD SEE IT!
SO WHAT ARE YOU WAITING FOR?
DO YOU LOVE HER?
YES! GIGGLE
DO YOU LOVE HER?
OH YEAH!
THEN WHAT ARE YOU WAITING FOR ?!

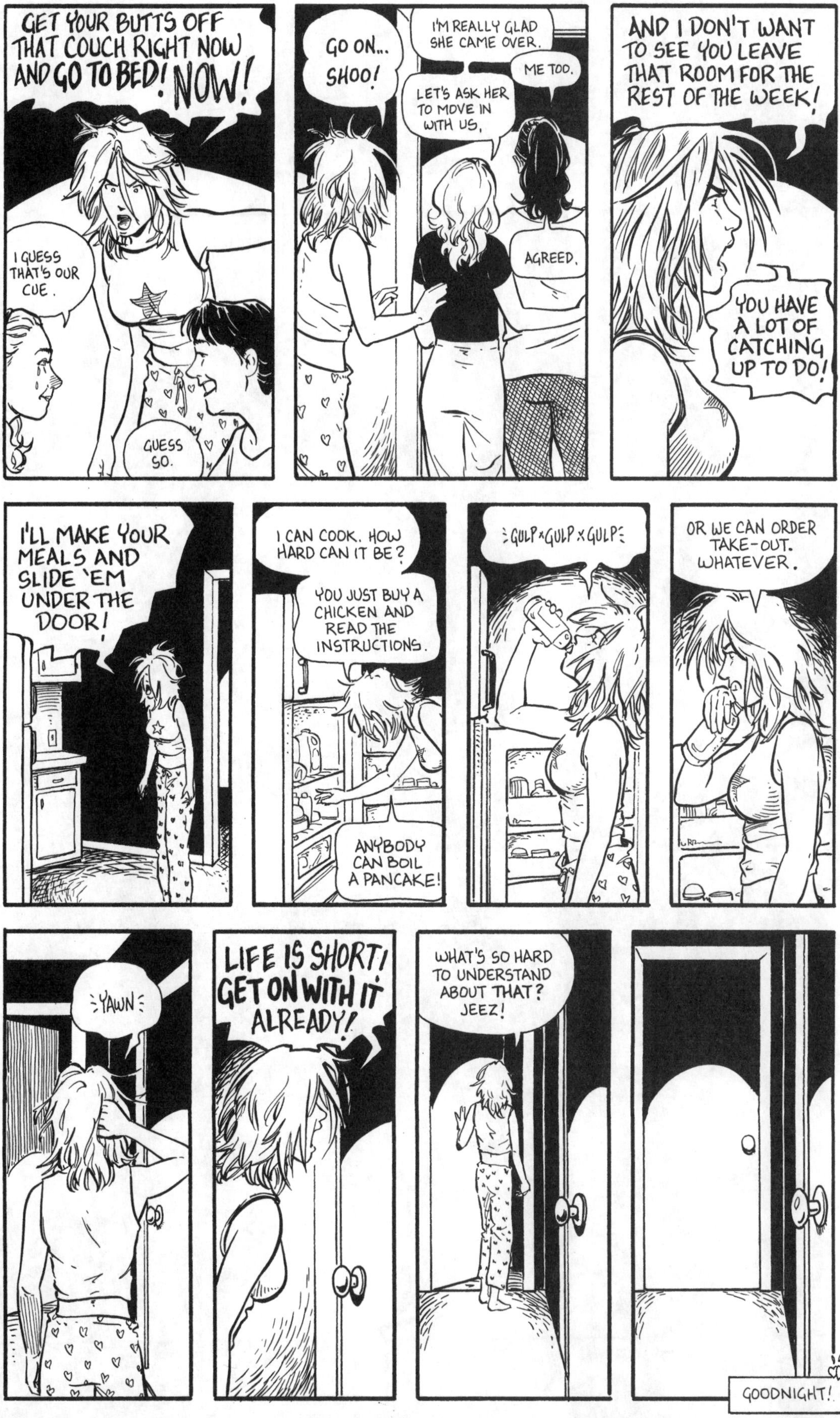
GET YOUR BUTTS OFF THAT COUCH RIGHT NOW AND GO TO BED! NOW!
I GUESS THAT'S OUR CUE.
GUESS SO.
GO ON... SHOO!
I'M REALLY GLAD SHE CAME OVER.
ME TOO.
LET'S ASK HER TO MOVE IN WITH US.
AGREED.
AND I DON'T WANT TO SEE YOU LEAVE THAT ROOM FOR THE REST OF THE WEEK!
YOU HAVE A LOT OF CATCHING UP TO DO!
I'LL MAKE YOUR MEALS AND SLIDE 'EM UNDER THE DOOR!
I CAN COOK. HOW HARD CAN IT BE?
YOU JUST BUY A CHICKEN AND READ THE INSTRUCTIONS.
ANYBODY CAN BOIL A PANCAKE!
GULP GULP GULP
OR WE CAN ORDER TAKE-OUT. WHATEVER.
YAWN
LIFE IS SHORT! GET ON WITH IT ALREADY!
WHAT'S SO HARD TO UNDERSTAND ABOUT THAT? JEEZ!
GOODNIGHT!

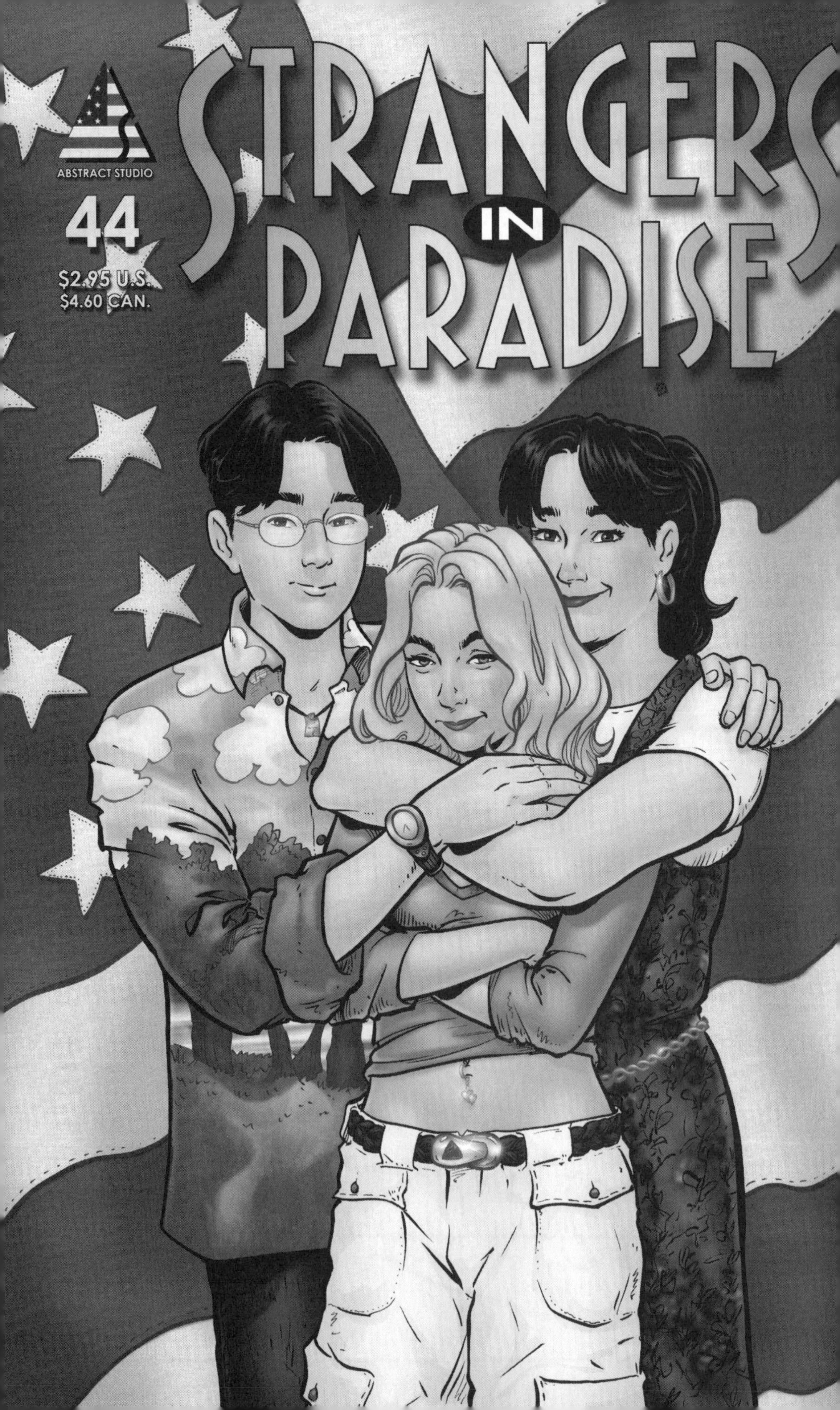

ABSTRACT STUDIO
44
$2.95 U.S.
$4.60 CAN.
STRANGERS IN PARADISE

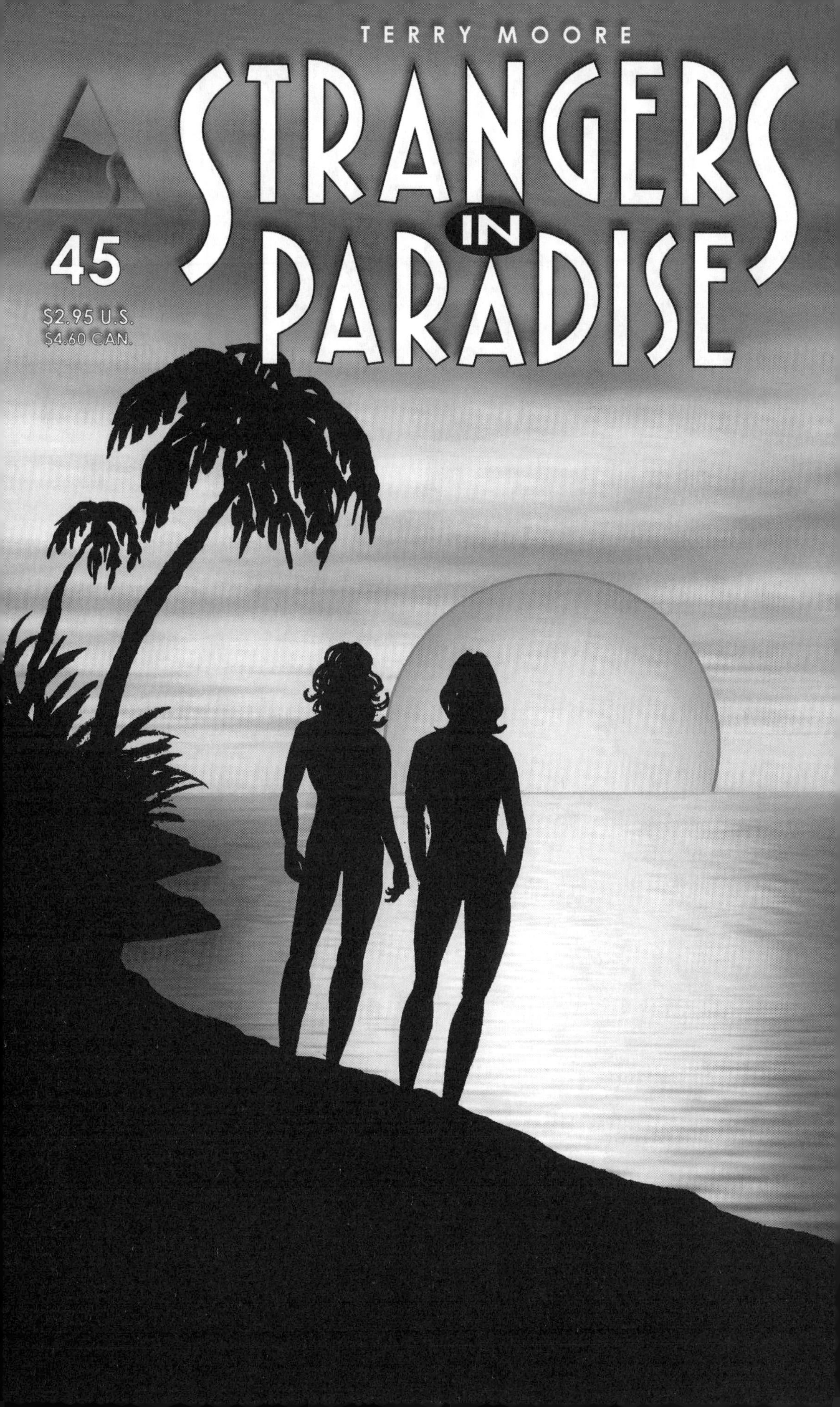
TERRY MOORE
STRANGERS IN PARADISE
45
$2.95 U.S.
$4.60 CAN.

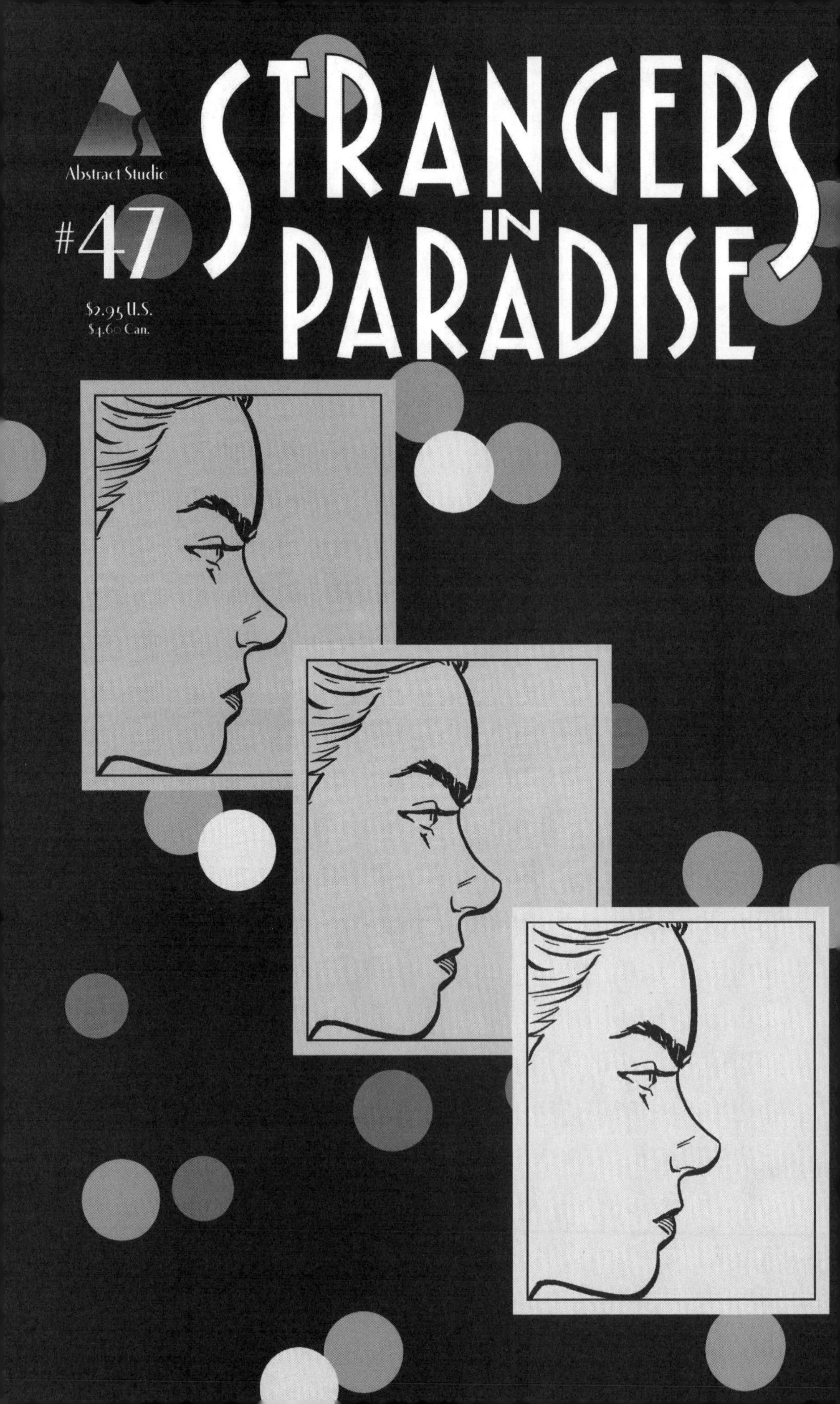
Abstract Studio
#47
$2.95 U.S.
$4.60 Can.
STRANGERS
IN
PARADISE

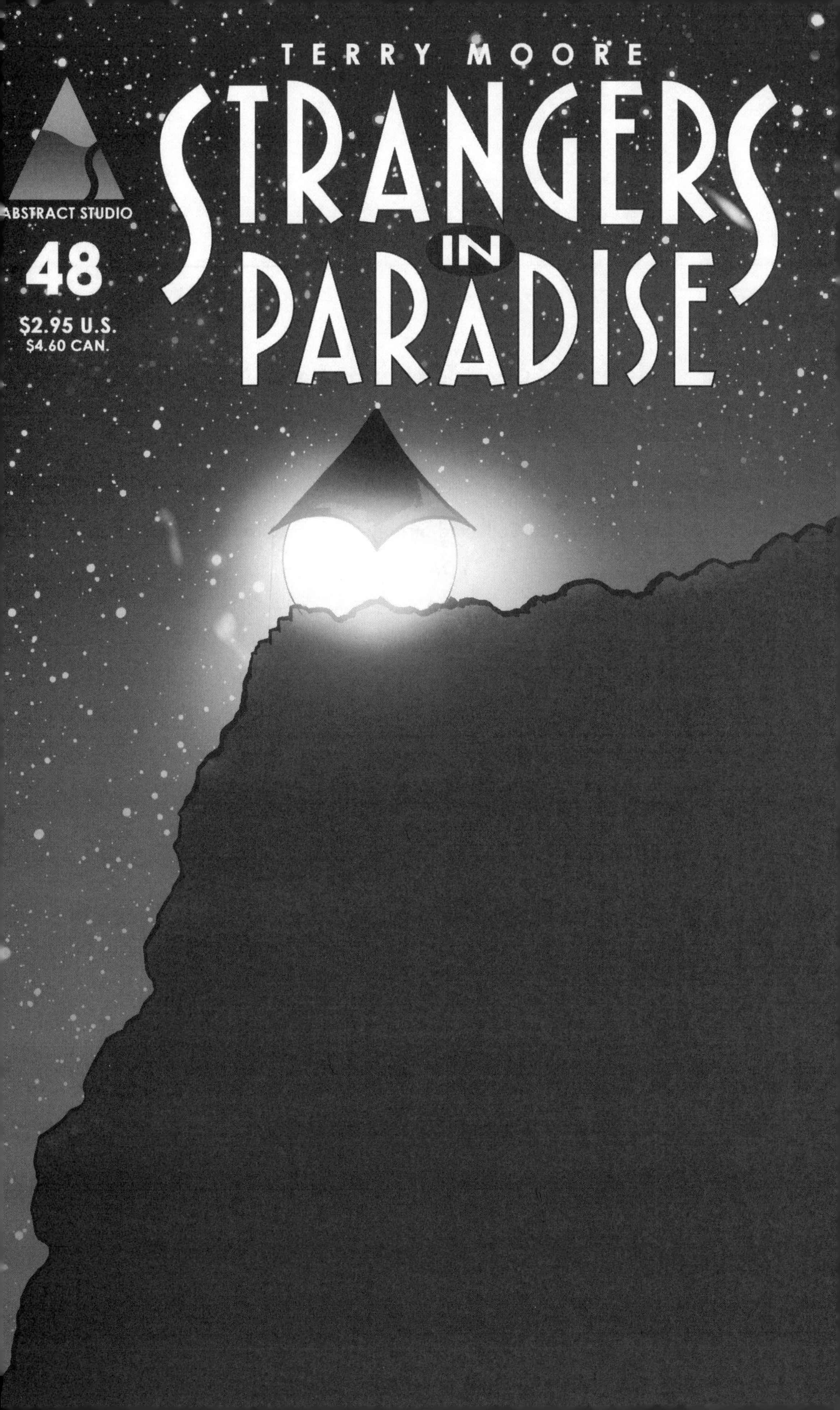
TERRY MOORE
STRANGERS IN PARADISE
ABSTRACT STUDIO
48
$2.95 U.S.
$4.60 CAN.

Other Books by Terry Moore

The Collected Strangers In Paradise

I Dream of You

It's A Good Life

Love Me Tender

Immortal Enemies

High School

Sanctuary

My Other Life

Child Of Rage

Tropic Of Desire